CW01498451

Aln

Kendall Feaver received the Judges' Award at the 2015
Bruntwood Prize for Playwriting, Best New Play at
the 2018 UK Theatre Awards, and the 2019 NSW and
Victorian Premier's Prizes for Drama for her play, *The
Almighty Sometimes* (Royal Exchange, Manchester;
Griffin Theatre Company, Sydney). Stage adaptations
include: *My Brilliant Career* by Miles Franklin (Belvoir
St Theatre, Sydney) and *Ballet Shoes* by Noel Streatfeild
(National Theatre, London). Kendall has written on invited
attachments at the National Theatre and Bush Theatre.
She was the 2019 Philip Parsons Fellow at Belvoir Street
Theatre, and an inaugural member of the Genesis Almeida
New Playwrights, Big Plays programme (2019/20).

KENDALL FEAVER

Alma Mater

faber

First published in 2024
by Faber and Faber Limited
The Bindery, 51 Hatton Garden
London, EC1N 8HN

Typeset by Brighton Gray
Printed and bound in the UK by CPI Group (Ltd), Croydon CR0 4YY

'Window' by Forugh Farrokhzad, translated by Elizabeth T. Gray, Jr.,
from *Let Us Believe in the Beginning of the Cold Season*, copyright © 2022
by Elizabeth T. Gray, Jr. (translation). Compilation copyright © 2022 by New
Directions Publishing. Used by permission of New Directions Publishing Corp.

A CIP record for this book
is available from the British Library

ISBN 978-0-571-39257-5

2 4 6 8 10 9 7 5 3 1

An earlier version of this play was performed at Griffin Theatre Company on 5 November 2021 at the SBW Stables Theatre, Sydney. A significantly revised and new version was produced and performed at the Almeida Theatre, London, on 11 June 2024.

Leila Bahrami Nathalie Armin
Nikki Stewart Phoebe Campbell
Paige Hutson Liv Hill
Gerald (Ghazali) Amir Liam Lau-Fernandez
Michael Danfield Nathaniel Parker
Jo Mulligan Lia Williams
Tamara Beade Susannah Wise

Director Polly Findlay
Set Designer Vicki Mortimer
Costume Designer Fay Fullerton
Lighting Designer Jessica Hung Han Yun
Sound Designer Ian Dickinson
Composer and Vocal Artist Alev Lenz
Musical Director Toby Higgins
Movement Director Shelley Maxwell
Casting Director Amy Ball CDG
Costume Supervisor Kate Hemstock
Dialect Coach Salvatore Sorce
Dramatherapist Wabriya King
Assistant Director Connie Treves

Characters

Jo (Josephine) Mulligan
fifty-six, white, British, possibly American, Australian or New Zealander. Regardless, spent most of her adult life based in England.

Michael Danfield
sixty-three, white, British

Nikki (Nicole) Stewart
twenty, dual heritage, English

Paige Hutson
eighteen, white, Welsh, possibly Northern Irish or Scottish

Gerald (Ghazali) Amir
twenty, Malay

Leila Bahrami
fifty-six, born in Iran, moved to the UK aged eleven

Tamara Beade
forty-eight, white, British, middle-class

Setting

A fictional residential college situated on the grounds of a very old and very elite British university.

ALMA MATER

I thought too that, at fifty, I might have forgotten what it was like to be a young woman out in the world, constantly the focus of men's sexual attraction . . . Worst of all, I wondered whether I had become like one of those emotionally scarred men who boast to their sons, 'I got the strap at school, and it didn't do me any harm.'

Helen Garner, *The First Stone: Some Questions on Sex and Power* (1992)

'she needs a good dicking, good luck finding it though'

'fuck you feminist fucks you already have equality'

'Someone needs to rape that bitch . . .'

'These dumb whores could use a Max Hardcore throatfuck session, cures any feminism guaranteed.'

Comments left on the YouTube videos of activists. As quoted in Kate Harding, *Asking for It: The Alarming Rise of Rape Culture* (2015)

You are the cause, I am the effect . . . If you think I was spared, came out unscathed, that today I ride off into the sunset, while you suffer the greatest blow, you are mistaken. Nobody wins.

Chanel Miller's Victim Impact Statement.
Read in court, then published online at BuzzFeed News
(2016) and then *Know My Name: A Memoir* (2019)

and then Jen showed me the spot
where the man with the knife
might have killed her and
now she comes to visit because
she says a place like this needs regular care.
There ought to have been a crouching beast
of a monument. Or snake pits. Or Dante's river
of fire and blood. But it was an everyday
kind of spot. Sunning itself by the roadside
it continued placid, mute as the dirt next door.
Jen had brought a picnic. We drank lemonade.

Cynthia White, 'She said stop here',
first appeared in *CALYX* (2017), published in
*Grabbed: Poets & Writers on Sexual Assault,
Empowerment & Healing* (2020)

Notes

The action takes place in a variety of locations.
These do not need to be more than suggested.

Each scene begins and ends abruptly.

A dash at the end of a line (–) indicates a slight overlap,
a sharp interruption and/or a rapid conversation without
space for breath. A forward slash (/) indicates the point
where a longer overlap occurs. These are offers only. Pacing
and delivery are yours to play with . . .

Notes on Voices

The Voices exist to provide an abstract or intangible sense
of online discussion and as texture or underscore only.
The extent to which they are embodied by the ensemble
of actors and the specifics of delivery (i.e. pace, overlap,
content) are all flexible, but the intent is that choral music
may play some significant part . . .

*This text went to press before the end of rehearsals and so
may differ slightly from the play as performed.*

Act One

Jo appears. A commencement speech. One year earlier.

Jo 'Cunts.' 'Dear Cunts.' That's how it began. A single typewritten page which slipped under the door of every new female student at this college.

(*Reading.*) 'Dear Cunts, Quims, Boxes and Holes. Your presence at this hitherto male-only institution compels us to treat you as our enemy. To maintain peace, several changes must be made. One, when eating in the dining hall, the upper part of your body must remain naked to the human eye. Two, your services as cooks, cleaners, bed-makers and bed-warmers must be available at all times.'

I confess . . . it made me laugh. Not at the letter's humour – which was underdeveloped, at best – but rather, its confidence. Its sheer audacity. I've always believed – continue to believe – that every attempt at conciliation, no matter how dim-witted, deserves some acknowledgement. In 1986, of course, this meant writing a note and then stapling it to the college noticeboard.

(*Reading.*) 'Dear Pricks, Cocks, Peckers and Bellends. Thank you for your letter of welcome. The pursuit of harmony is a collective mission deeply cherished by us all. Your letter, however, indicates you may never have known the ecstatic beauty of shared love that can exist between a man and a woman. To broaden your comprehension, I have placed several copies of Masters and Johnson's *Human Sexual Inadequacy* on reserve in the college library. I encourage you all to delve into its wisdom . . .'

Jo's office. Start of the current academic year.
   Jo and Michael, mid-argument. Jo, a perpetual multitasker, tries to eat or assemble her lunch, rarely skipping a beat in the conversation.

Michael No. *No.* No no no no no Josie, absolutely not –

Jo It's one room, Michael –

Michael Which requires us to repurpose the games room –

Jo They already have a common room, not to mention the college bar –

Michael This is a place of *learning.* We create futures here. We enrich minds. Last time I checked; we were not in the business of providing religious services –

Jo We have an eighty-seat chapel –

Michael Because the college was founded in the *Christian* tradition. The building is Grade I listed – the chapel is the oldest part of it –

Jo I'm aware – thank you –

Michael It also happens to have one of the finest gothic interiors in the country –

Jo Yes, but it's not like the kids use it to pray in.

   Beat.

Michael What do they use it for?

Jo Nothing. Forget I said anything –

Michael Josie –

Jo Well, if you must know, these days, it's mainly used for fucking in.

Michael Josephine –

Jo And before you blame any negligence on my part, it's been happening since the mid-1980s and is still, I'm told, a firm and favourite college tradition.

Michael The chapel has the only Arthur Thomas organ in the country.

Jo I don't think they care, Michael.

Michael The windows are by Ferguson and Plank. *Ferguson and Plank.* The 1825 refurbishment was their first-ever commission –

Jo So it should thrill you to know how thoroughly it's being enjoyed –no, I'm serious. Think of everyone who's been pressed up against the walls or laid out behind the pulpit. CEOs. Entrepreneurs. Artists. Even a certain high-profile politician –

Michael Josie, a chapel is supposed to be *sacrosanct* –

Jo Riiight –

Michael A place for quiet reflection, and – and singing, and – and *prayer* –

Jo Michael. When the Board hired me, you specifically asked me to diversify the student population –

Michael Well, yes, but –

Jo And now we have twenty-two students here who practise a religion *other* than Christianity –

Michael And we're very impressed by that, well done you –

Jo And some of these students might also like a place for quiet reflection, singing, prayer – and if the Board won't approve a separate multi-faith prayer room, then I will ask that we return to my first and preferred option: that we strip the chapel of anything Jesus-Christ-specific –

Michael Strip the chapel, Josie – ?!

7

Jo And we make it available to all.

Beat.

Michael Where do you propose we get the money for this room – ?

Jo I've already sorted it. Last year's budget had two hundred and fifty thousand set aside for 'general wear and tear' –

Michael Yes . . .

Jo A quarter of a million pounds . . . for 'general wear and tear?' What the fuck are they doing –

Michael Three years ago, I believe, a group of first years engaged in some kind of vomiting competition in the junior common room, so we had to re-carpet –

Jo And we paid for it?

Michael Of course.

Jo Of course?!

Michael It's all part of the experience, Josie. One of the main draws of the place, if I'm honest with you. A little bit of silly behaviour is to be . . . well . . . expected . . . encouraged even.

Jo I'm taking fifty.

Michael Josie, that is not how we –

Jo I'm taking fifty thousand pounds, which still leaves two hundred thousand for 'silly behaviour', we are creating a multi-faith prayer room, and when I go into that meeting, you will support me on this, do you understand me –

A knock. Jo moves to get the door.

Michael We're still talking, Josie, don't you dare answer that –

Jo She made an appointment –

Nikki appears.

Hello – Nikki –

Nikki / Oh . . . hi . . .

Michael Josie, I refuse to be bustled – Hello Nikki, lovely to see you again –

Nikki / Um . . . you too.

Jo I'm sorry, did you just use the word *bustled*?

Michael What's . . . What's wrong with bustled – ?

Nikki Do you want me to wait outside, or –

Michael That would be lovely, dear, I just need five more minutes –

Jo (*on her phone, typing*) No, Nikki, you stay exactly where you are – (*Reading.*) 'Bustle. Late Middle English. To move in a noisy, energetic and often *obtrusive* manner' –

Michael Right. I'm leaving to speak to your secretary –

Jo (*reading*) / 'Bustle. Later definition, eighteenth-century, a pad or framework worn under a woman's skirt to provide further rotundity or prominence to' –

Michael (*overlapping*) I am leaving to speak to your secretary, Josie, and I hope, between Louisa and I, we're able to find some room in your very busy schedule for an appointment later today –

Jo Wonderful –

Michael Later today, Josie –

Jo I'm looking forward to it.

Michael exits.

(*Indicating her phone.*) 'Artificial intelligence chatbot.' My goddaughter taught me how to use it last week. Of course

I don't condone its use in academia, but as a random facts dispenser – absolutely marvellous. Now, what can I do for you? You wanted to speak to me about something?

Nikki Yes.

Jo And is this the kind of conversation we can have while I eat my lunch?

Nikki Uh –

Jo No? Yes?

Nikki Yes.

Jo Okay –

Nikki I think – ?

Jo Well, let's see, shall we?

Jo dives into her food.

(*Not unkindly.*) Go on . . . I'm listening.

Nikki Okay. Um. So . . .

Nikki takes a deep breath, then launches in:

Last night, um . . . I was in the common room um . . . organising the Welcome Packs, and uh . . . there were a bunch of guys in there, um . . . third years, I – I think they were all members of the social committee – ?

Jo (*moving her along*) Okay –

Nikki They were supposed to be creating an events schedule for Freshers Week, but instead, they were, um . . . They were looking up pictures of girls on the internet, which wouldn't actually be that unusual at all, except I realised . . . I realised the girls are tomorrow's incoming students.

She pauses to allow Jo to take this in.

You gave all the Student Reps a list of names, remember? Well, I think they used that list to look up all the girl's social media profiles, most likely to check how uh . . . hot or um . . . not . . . she is, and uh . . . yeah . . . I uh . . . I thought you should know.

Beat.

Jo Why?

Nikki *Why?*

Jo Why should I know?

Nikki Sorry, I . . . I don't um –

Jo Is it so I can have a general awareness, or because you want me to do something about it?

Nikki Um . . . do something about it – ?

Jo What, in particular, would you like me to do?

Nikki I don't know . . . Maybe you could talk to them, like, like firmly, or –

Jo Take a few things away from them? Their positions on the Social Committee, for example –

Nikki I mean . . . probably not, but if you think it's necessary –

Jo And what reason should I give them?

Nikki I don't know, that, um . . . that this is a residential college? Which is supposed to offer a safe and secure um . . . learning . . . environment? But actions like this might make new students, particularly, particularly female students, feel slightly . . . I don't know . . . uncomfortable?

Jo Did you try telling them this yourself?

Nikki Well . . . no, but –

Jo Why not? You just explained it better than I could?

Beat.

Nikki Sorry, I . . . I guess, I . . . I guess I thought this was going to be a different kind of conversation –

Jo The ability to navigate difficult conversations is an essential journalistic skill, Nikki – no – an essential *human* skill – and you are not going to learn that skill if you keep asking me to / intervene in relatively minor instances of . . .

Nikki Okay, but I haven't . . . *twice*, I . . . Okay, um, 'relatively minor' – ?

Jo I'm on your side, Nikki; I'm just . . . I'm suggesting a change in approach.
  This? Whatever it is you're doing . . . ? It doesn't work. Men hate it. Women hate it. Every single sub-faction of feminism hates it. Try it too long, you'll find yourself locked in a room with a whole bunch of us, everyone tearing strips off the other because no one – and I mean *no one* – can sustain the many, *many* rules you've set –

Nikki (*genuinely*) So what do I . . . What do I do, because –

Jo Use your wits. Use that big ol' brain in that extraordinarily beautiful head of yours. I know; why don't you download pictures of all the boys on the Social Committee – staple them to the noticeboard? Then you could have the student body rate their attractiveness on a scale of one to ten –

Nikki You're giving me permission to –

Jo This is your last year as an undergrad, Nikki. Put a hat on a statue, cling-film a toilet – I don't care what it is, just – just make sure it costs less than two hundred thousand pounds –

Nikki What – ?

Jo A joke, a joke, I'm sorry.

Beat.

I want you to try and have some fun this year . . . okay?

Beat.

. . . Okay?

Nikki (*smiling, charmed*) Okay.

Nikki is obviously desperate to discuss something else.

Jo Is there something (else) –

Nikki Yes, actually.

Nikki takes out a photocopied article from her backpack and hesitates.

Um –

SCENE THREE

Paige's new college bedroom.

Paige (*singing the Harry Potter theme song*) Da daaa da-da-daaaa da daaa da . . . da . . . da-da-da da . . . daaaaa . . . Please tell me you know what Harry Potter is –

Gerald No, I . . . I've seen the movies, yeah –

Paige Okay, so . . . Hogwarts . . . right? Don't you think it looks like Hogwarts?

Gerald Um, maybe –

Paige Come on, the fireplaces, and the . . . the castle walls and the . . . the cobbled streets, it's like going to a *real* university, like . . . like a *proper* university –

Gerald Well Hogwarts isn't a university, or uh, real so –

Paige Yeah, I . . . / I know . . .

Gerald And the college has fireplaces because it's old. Six hundred and seventy-seven years old –

Paige Yeah, I . . . / I kind of knew that too . . .

Gerald And just between you and me, um . . . try not to be, like . . . try not to be *awed* by it, okay – ?

Paige Oh – okay –

Gerald But you don't need to make fun of it either –

Paige I wasn't making fun of it –

Gerald It's normal, just . . . pretend all of this is like . . . completely normal –

Paige Sure, like it's totally normal to wear a wizard cape to dinner –

Gerald Gowns. They're called gowns, and . . . and it's actually kind of an important tradition, so –

Nikki (*entering*) Ghazali –

Gerald Nikki – hi –

Nikki Why are there no event schedules in the Welcome Packs?

Gerald Because I'm going door to door passing them out now.

Nikki Yeah, but . . . why aren't they already *in* the Welcome Packs – ?

Gerald Jo-Ma suggested we maybe wait until after all the parents had gone before we hand them out – ?

Nikki What? / *Why?*

Gerald (*to Paige*) Jo-Ma is the Master here –

Paige Yeah, I –

14

Gerald I was the one who actually came up with her nickname because her first name is Jo and her last name is Mulligan, but she's also the Master, so –

Paige So 'Jo-Ma', yeah –

Gerald She's great. Last year, she gave this commencement dinner speech in which she said the actual C-word, like, like the worst word you can think of; she said it, and during a *formal* dinner –

Paige Wow – okay –

Gerald And then she used like three other different words for it – 'quims, boxes, holes' – it was *amazing* – you definitely picked the right college –

Paige Oh – great –

Nikki Yeah, it's the only college where a student has actually been murdered, so . . .

Beat.

Gerald Fuck . . . Nikki –

Nikki Sorry, I –

Gerald It's her first day –

Nikki Yeah, I . . . I actually don't even know why I said that –

Paige Someone was murdered here – ?!

Gerald Yeah, great job, Nikki – 'Welcome to college, Paige' –

Nikki It was like thirty-something-almost-forty years ago, so –

Paige In this building, or –

Nikki No –   **Gerald** *No* –

Nikki It was somewhere near the edge of the sports ground –

Gerald Nikki – !

Nikki Which is like several hundred metres away from the building, and hardly anyone knows about it, and I shouldn't have said anything, and . . . Hi, I'm Nikki . . .

Paige Paige – hi –

Gerald Okay, you've reminded me about the schedule, so –

Nikki (*ignoring him, to Paige*) What are you studying?

Paige Um . . . Computer Science – ?

Nikki Whoa. Why Computer Science – ?

Gerald Come on, Nikki, / she just got here, you don't like . . . You don't need to interrogate her . . .

Paige I guess because none of my friends wanted to take Computer Science for A-levels, but all the boys did, and I just . . . I really hated the idea that instead of learning a language responsible for building like – like any system imaginable, all the girls just wanted to take, like . . . like beginner Spanish, so . . .

   Beat.

You're taking Spanish, aren't you –

Nikki Not . . . beginner Spanish –

Paige Oh . . . God . . .   **Gerald** (*delighted, to himself*)
                                  Holy shit . . .

Nikki I also study Politics and Philosophy –

Paige Genuinely, I wasn't trying to offend you –

Nikki (*unfazed*) Creo que es realmente genial que sepas cómo programar –

Paige Um . . . what?

Nikki (*translation*) I think it's really cool that you know how to code.

Paige Oh . . . thanks, and –

But Nikki is already on to her next task –

Nikki (*to Gerald*) Please don't forget the / events schedules –

Gerald Events schedules – got it – yeah –

Paige (*calling after Nikki*) I'm uh . . . I'm really sorry if I kept Gerald from doing whatever it was he was supposed to be doing – ?

Nikki (*stopping*) Gerald?

Beat.

Gerald Yeah . . . Gerald . . . Gerry . . . (*To Paige.*) The guys call me Gerry –

Nikki 'Gerry' . . . okay –

Gerald (*to Paige*) Gerald's a nickname –

Nikki Except it's basically the same length as Ghazali –

Gerald There's nothing wrong with Gerald, Nikki –

Nikki There's nothing wrong with Ghazali – you can shorten it to Ghaz –

Gerald I like Gerald – !

Nikki It's the name of every old white man ever –

Gerald Really – 'every old white man ever' –

Nikki There is not a single person under the age of sixty-five called Gerald –

Gerald Sure there is –

Nikki Okay, you find me an eight-month-old Gerald; prove me wrong –

Gerald (*shaking on it*) Challenge accepted –

Paige Sorry, are you guys like . . . together, or . . . ?

Nikki What – ?!

Gerald *No . . . no* –

Nikki No – definitely not – gross –

Gerald Um . . . *gross*, Nikki – ?

Nikki (*to Paige*) We're friends – *just* friends –

Gerald Correction: used to be friends.

Nikki Well that's clarity at least –

Gerald Come on, Nikki – I meant until you called me gross –

Nikki (*to Paige*) Gerry and I – we spent most of first year hanging out together, but then halfway through second year, he discovered polo shirts and decided he was too cool to play video games with a girl, so –

Gerald / Whoa – okay – that's not . . .

Paige Wait . . . Do you game?

Nikki Um. Sometimes? Not like . . . 'religiously', or –

Paige I game so much my mum refused to let me bring my headset to college.

Nikki Well that's the thing about college: you don't have to listen to your parents any more, so –

Paige Yeah, but she made me promise her, like, like while I'm here, I'm under explicit instructions to only engage in activities more or less based in the real world, so –

Nikki You think this is the real world?! Fucking *Game of Thrones* / Middle-Earth –

Paige It's like *Hogwarts* – I know!

Beat.

Gerald Great. Well it was nice knowing you, Paige –

Nikki I'm sorry, Gerry, I didn't realise you were still here –

Gerald It's Freshers Week, no one should be talking about video games –

Nikki No, instead you should sample the diverse array of events the Social Committee has set for you – (*Reading the events schedule.*) Oh, what the *fuck*, Ghazali –

Gerald (*to Paige*) I'll see you tonight, yeah – ?

Paige Yeah – okay – maybe –

Nikki Joma said you needed to give the girls some options this year – !

Gerald (*leaving*) They have options, Nikki –

Nikki (*calling after him*) Yeah, lace, leather or latex!

Gerald exits.

Paige I uh . . . I actually think tonight's theme is kind of clever?

Nikki 'What were you wearing when the police raided the brothel?' That's the theme, that's the actual theme –

Paige I mean we could totally subvert it? Brothel madam . . . female pimp . . . all out dominatrix suit and uh . . . whip.

Nikki Yay . . . 'options'.

Paige Or . . . I don't have to go at all, like . . . maybe we could hang out, or –

Nikki No – no – you should definitely go. You need to spend three years with these people; you should probably make friends with at least some of them –

Paige Oh – okay. No – sure. Yeah.

Nikki He likes you. By the way.

Paige Who? *Gerald – ?!*

Nikki Gerald, Gerry – whatever his name is –

Paige Uhh why would he like me?

Nikki Uhhh I don't know, have you looked in a mirror lately – ?

Paige What – ?

Nikki You're really pretty –

Paige Noooo, I'm not –

Nikki But you are – like – you really actually are –

Paige No, I'm really actually not –

Nikki Can I teach you something?

Paige Um . . . okay –

Nikki Brace yourself though because all the wisdom you're about to inherit, this is like . . . groundbreaking stuff –

Paige Okay –

Nikki So whenever someone compliments you . . . even if you don't believe it . . . you have to resist the urge to deny it, and instead, you say this one thing and one thing only . . .

Paige . . . What?

Nikki 'Thank you.' Paige, I think you're really pretty.

Paige Thank you. I think you're really pretty too –

Nikki Nooo, you don't have to compliment *me* –

Paige Aren't you just supposed to say, 'Thank you'?

Nikki Thank you. Even though I know you were just –

Paige Hey!

Nikki Thank you. (*Then, genuinely.*) Thank you.

The college chapel. Night.
  Jo, several glasses of wine in. Michael, also partaking, keeps a close eye on the entrance, troubled by the sounds of a party nearby . . .

Jo (*reading*) 'Don't go out alone. Don't walk into the night. Never stray from the well-lit path. For the last two weeks, this frayed and tattered advice has been offered up as if women have never heard these warnings before –'

Michael Where exactly are they doing it in here – ?

Jo Michael, focus, please –

Michael It's not near the lectern, is it? Because the marble floor in that section of the chapel – *that's* original –

Jo What I have in my hand is original. An original Josephine Mulligan by-line – not Jo – not Josie – *Josephine Mulligan* – nineteen, maybe twenty – Michael, this is riveting stuff –

Michael Okay –okay – I'm sorry – I'm listening –

Jo 'But what our mothers and police officers and university officials fail to understand is –'

  Leila enters with bags of takeaway.

Leila Fucking soy sauce / fucking salty shitting fucking fermented fucking –

Jo (*kissing her, diving into the bags*) Leila! Goddess! Angel!

21

Leila I *knew* this was going to happen. You said Chinese food – I had a vision – and that vision was of me scrubbing soy sauce out of these trousers. Does anyone have anything I can blot this with – ?

Michael (*handing her stain remover*) Here . . . stain remover.

Leila (*kissing him*) Ah, thank you, azizam –

Jo You just carry that around, do you – ?

Michael I'm a red wine drinker.

Leila He's a red wine drinker –

Jo Of course! Silly me!

Leila I thought we were supposed to be having dinner in your office?

Jo We were.

Leila And? What happened?

Jo What happened is your red-wine-drinking husband stopped to have a conversation with a student.

Michael I didn't know he was a student. I thought, from behind, that he was the college chaplain.

Leila Why would you think he was the college chaplain – ?

Jo He was a student *dressed* as a college chaplain.

Leila Why was a student dressed as a college chaplain – ?

Michael *Exactly* –

Jo Party theme. 'What were you wearing when the police raided the brothel?' –

Leila Ahhh.

Jo Mostly pimps and prostitutes. But a few of the more inventive students came as celebrities or politicians –

Michael Or college chaplains –

Jo And now that Michael has realised there's a party in the junior common room and no *actual* chaplain on site, he's taken it upon himself to protect this sacred space from its most popular tradition . . .

Leila You mean the students like to . . .

Michael Apparently, yes.

Leila (*to Michael*) So . . . did you ever . . .

Michael No, Leila, I didn't.

Leila Why not – ?

Jo (*eating*) Because in his day, a chapel was considered sacrosanct –

Leila Riiight –

Jo A place for quiet reflection . . . singing . . . *prayer* –

Leila Michael, I'm not sure if you remember this, but thirty-three years ago, you decided to marry a Muslim woman –

Michael I'm aware –

Leila So if you're trying to gain favour with Our-God-in-Heaven, there are quite a few versions of him you've pissed off already –

Michael Yes, but you're not really Muslim, darling . . .

Leila No?

Michael Culturally . . . maybe –

Leila (*to Jo*) 'Culturally' – !

Michael But not practising. You haven't set foot in a mosque since 1979.

Leila And you're not a practising Anglican, and yet, somehow, here I am, ferrying supplies as you prepare for a siege of the college chapel –

Jo Leila, what would you do if a student came to you with a shampoo bottle full of spunk? Sorry . . . sorry . . . 'alleged' spunk. What would you do if a student came to you with a shampoo bottle that is – *allegedly* – full of spunk?

Leila Did this happen?

Jo Maybe . . . I'm not sure. Halfway through last year, this student, Nicole – Nikki – she came to my office . . . with a bottle of shampoo. She'd heard laughing in the bathroom, and then, later, some guy came up to her in the dining hall, sniffed her hair – cue more laughter from the boys. So of course Nikki is wondering if they'd put something in it, but the problem is . . . well, it's not like someone defecating in a shoe. Semen is sort of . . . well, it's roughly the same consistency as the shampoo itself –

Michael Is it?

Jo If you put the two of them side by side, you'd struggle to tell the difference –

Leila Why didn't you give it to me?

Beat.

Jo I'm sorry. I didn't realise that was something you'd want.

Leila I have an entire laboratory at my disposal. I could have tested it.

Jo Oooh she would have loved that . . . little CSI on her Pantene Pro-V . . .

Leila Or maybe she just wanted some help?

Jo No . . . no . . . there's always a little too much . . . pre-emptive triumph. She's so earnest, so . . . so *desperate*, sometimes. I like her. No – I *really* like her. She's profoundly annoying, of course, but at least she cares about something – I mean, something other than what to wear to the next college social. And she's clever. One of our best students. She wants to be a journalist, and yes, I've already warned her that magazines and newspapers might not actually exist by the time she enters the job market but see . . . she's thought about that too. She has a blog . . . *a blog* . . . remember those? Her peers are all posting topless pictures of themselves with nothing but a series of emojis covering their nipples, and there Nikki is . . . practising her long form. She's not waiting for the *Guardian* to hand her an opinion column; she's just . . . given it to herself. I feel . . . proud, maybe? I don't know why, but I do.

Leila and Michael share a look.

What? No . . . No, I wasn't that annoying, was I?

Michael You were a little self-righteous –

Jo No, I wasn't –

Michael Standing on that podium, screaming into that scratchy old megaphone, what did you use to say – 'The right to resist – !'

Leila *and* **Jo** To exist.

Jo The right to *exist*.

Jo takes out the article and reads:

'If a woman walks home and violence befalls her, the inevitable strictures will follow. What was she wearing? Where was she going. How *dare* she exist in a place at night.'

She passes it over to Leila.

Nikki dug it out of the archives. She wants to write about it. What's changed, what hasn't, where we fucked up, I'm sure . . .

Michael Alison Welsh. I hadn't heard that name in years.

Leila You wouldn't, would you? The memorial is barely the size of a postcard –

Jo *And* it's hidden under a tree –

Leila It's also nowhere near the football pitch –

Jo Well, the college can hardly put a memorial in the middle of a sports ground, Leila –

Leila I never thought you'd put it in the *middle* of the pitch; I just thought . . . maybe the general vicinity?

Michael It's a bit morbid, isn't it? Playing rugby or football next to a memorial for a murdered student –

Leila Not as morbid as playing rugby or football on top of the place she died. Every time I walk past there, see some sweaty spotty teenager kicking a ball . . . oblivious . . . It makes me want to scream.

Michael So why don't you do something about it?

Jo Leila? *Our* Leila? Raise her head above the parapet?

Leila And what's that supposed to mean?

Jo You're not political. You don't have a strong opinion about anything –

Leila I don't think that's true –

Jo (*to Michael*) I had to educate your wife on the revolution that happened in her own country –

Leila You didn't have to educate me, I experienced it first-hand –

Jo No you didn't. Your entire family flew out of there months before the worst of it – first class tickets – British Airways – you couldn't have been more than eleven years old –

Leila I built a life in a country that wasn't my own. My mother is in a decent British nursing home that I pay for. I run the largest research laboratory on campus, I've birthed and raised two daughters –

Jo I thought you were going to cure cancer – when's that happening?

Leila You were going to be Prime Minister. Or work for the UN. Look at you now . . . glorified innkeeper –

Michael (*warning*) Ladies –

Jo Better paid. With a secretary called Louisa. Free meals, free accommodation, a giant working fireplace in my office –

Leila Five-hundred-plus students to worship you –

Jo And I them. They're life, Leila, *real* life – a phone-trapped version of it, sure – but even that they inherited from us – and though my tolerance for sentiment stops somewhere short of calling them 'the remaining hope for all of human civilisation' – that is exactly what they are, and why I'm here, and one day, maybe, I'll return to phoning in five a.m. articles from some shitty-Eastern-European-hotel-room slash shitty-Washington-hotel-room, but until then, I happen to know the Chair of a prestigious residential college, and he was stupid enough to give me a job –

Michael You're welcome –

Jo I'm grateful –

Michael You know what they call you, right –

Jo It's brilliant, isn't it –

Michael 'Jo-Ma' –

Jo *Jo*ma – emphasis on the 'Jo' –

Michael No, I'm pretty sure the emphasis is on the 'Ma' –

Leila Alison's mother died last year.

    Beat.

Jo Leila . . . Why didn't you tell me – ?

Leila I went to her funeral, and . . . and I realised . . . Alison was an only child. Her father died before she did, so . . . who does Alison have to remember her now?'

Jo gets down on the floor, wraps herself around Leila.

Jo You. She has you.

Leila leans in, allows herself to be held.

Leila I can't remember anything important. Her favourite food was tinned pineapple. She had an irrational fear of garden hedgehogs – I'm hardly an archive of knowledge –

Michael (*reciting*)

یک چند به کودکی به استاد شدیم

(Yek chand be koodaki be ostad shodim)

یک چند به استادی خود شاد شدیم

(Yek chand be ostadi khod shad shodim)

پایان سخن شنو که ما را چه رسید

(Payan-e sokhan shenav ke ma ra cheh resid)

از خاک در آمدیم و بر باد شدیم

(Az khak dar amadim o bar baad shodim)

Jo (*overlapping*) English, Michael – English –

Leila (*translating*) 'Once, we were children learning. Some of our friends became the Masters. But listen to the end of us: we came from the soil, and, like dust, will be blown away by the wind.'

Michael Omar Khayyam.

Beat.

Jo What an uplifting poem, Michael, thank you for that.

Leila snort-laughs into her wine.

Michael Well the direct translation doesn't really do it justice –

Jo No no – bit of Persian apocalyptic poetry – that's exactly what your grieving wife needed to hear –

Leila (*to Jo*) Good pronunciation, you have to give him that –

Jo (*genuinely impressed*) Was it – ?

Leila (*to Michael*) You've been practising . . .

Michael I have, actually.

Jo (*raising her glass*) Well . . . to Michael then.

Leila (*raising her glass*) To Michael.

Michael (*raising his glass*) To Alison.

Jo To Alison. Lover of pineapple, hater of hedgehogs –

Leila Jo –

Jo Beloved daughter. Cherished friend. The day we lost you, we began to mark our lives by all the things you've missed. But while we are still on this earth, and until we are all blown away by the wind . . . we remember.

Jo raises her glass to the heavens.

Michael (*now reading the article*) Alison Welsh. I wonder if I ever met her. Spoke to her, even.

Jo I sincerely doubt it, Michael.

Michael And why is that?

Jo / Because Alison . . .

Leila Because Alison was studying chemistry. With me.

Nikki's college room.

Nikki Berocca? Gatorade? Sometimes coconut water helps – ?

Paige No, honestly, it's okay –

Nikki I think I have ibuprofen somewhere –

Paige I've pretty sure I've already reached my maximum dose, so –

Nikki Caitlin next door keeps like twelve jars of pickles under her desk – ?

Paige Pickles – ?

Nikki *In brine.* Has to be in brine, she says – restores lost sodium, electrolytes – wait here, I'll go get one for you –

Paige No, um, can I just . . .

Nikki realises Paige is crying. At the same time, so does Paige . . .

Shit, sorry, um –

Nikki It's okay –

Paige No, I – I don't even know why I –

Nikki First week is hard. Everyone pretends it isn't, because there are so many parties to go to, but after two or three of them, all you really want to do is just . . . go home . . . sleep in your own actual bed. It can really be confronting when you realise that your own actual bed is like –

Paige A four-and-a-half-hour drive away – ?

Nikki Exactly. But give it a few weeks, you'll start finding your people. You'll go to classes, you'll fight with your professors – you'll start having fun. And then you'll drive those four and a half hours to visit everyone at home, you'll be there five minutes, and trust me, you'll be desperate to drive all the way back –

Paige Um, do you uh . . . Do you know how I sign up for a doctor?

Nikki A doctor? You're hungover, Paige, you're not dying –

Paige I just . . . I thought it would be good to find a doctor, like, I've got a doctor, back at home. I've been with him since I was a baby, so I . . . I guess I don't actually know how to sign up for a new one –

Nikki Don't worry, it's easy –

Paige Okay, good –

Nikki There's a practice nearby; I'll take you next week if you like –

Paige Um, I really need to speak to someone soon, like . . . like before Wednesday?

Beat.

I . . . slept with someone. Last night.

Nikki That was –

Paige Quick, I know.

Nikki Who was it? I mean . . . if you don't mind me asking –

Paige No . . . no, it's fine, I just . . . I can't, um . . . I can't really remember his name?

Nikki Do you want to maybe . . . I don't know . . . describe him, or . . .

Paige Tall? Curly brown hair? When I first saw him, he was hanging out with Gerald –

Nikki Gerald – ?

Paige They're friends, I think –

Nikki Do you remember anything else – ?

Paige I think he mentioned he was into athletics or – or cycling / or something –

Nikki You slept with Aaron Beade?

Paige Is that a . . . Is that a bad thing?

Nikki No. It's kind of impressive, actually. A lot of girls really like him, so.

Paige (*relieved*) Oh . . . okay.

Nikki How was it?

Paige Um . . . good . . . I think.

Nikki You think –

Paige I think I may have passed out before the actual sex, / so . . .

Nikki What do you mean?

Paige I'm kind of . . . I'm kind of sore? And um. His um – sorry, this is really stupid and embarrassing and –

Nikki Paige –

Paige His stuff was inside me? And no matter how drunk I got, I know I would never let anyone have sex with me without a condom – anyway – I need the morning-after pill, but I googled it, and you have to take it within seventy-two hours, which brings me through to Wednesday, two a.m. . . . maybe. I'm not um . . . I'm not exactly sure what time he uh . . . Sorry, is that um . . . is that all too much information, or –

Nikki Paige, you need to tell someone.

Paige Yeah, I'm . . . I'm telling you –

Nikki No, I mean . . . I think you might need to tell someone who can actually do something about it –

Paige I don't need anyone to *do* anything / about it –

Nikki Paige, you were assaulted –

Paige Whoa okay.
Okay, *no.*
I was not . . . (*Lowering her voice.*) I was not *assaulted* –

Nikki Aaron had non-consensual sex with your body –

Paige Would you keep your voice down, please – !

Nikki Which is the textbook definition of rape.

Beat.

Have you already had a shower – ?

Paige Of course, I –

Nikki Whatever you do, don't wash your sheets or the clothes you were wearing –

Paige It was my first night here, Nikki, my – my *first* – what kind of . . . what kind of girl sleeps with someone their first night of university –

Nikki But you didn't sleep with someone, you were –

Paige Don't say that word, please!

Beat.

Look, I . . . I don't really remember anything, okay? And I'm pretty sure he was drunk too –

Nikki *So – ?*

Paige I'm a fresher. He's been here as long as you have –

Nikki And has probably been doing shit like this for the last two years –

Paige Nikki –

Nikki I *knew* this was going to happen –

33

Paige What are you talking about – ?

Nikki It's not 'relatively minor' behaviour when it results in actual *fucking* assault –

Paige Can you calm down please –

Nikki Why should I calm down?!

Paige Because it didn't happen to you, did it?!

Beat.

Nikki I'm sorry, I . . . Is there anything I can do, or –

Paige Right now, I just really don't want to be pregnant, so I need to see a doctor, and before Wednesday – Can you let me know how to do that? Please?

Nikki collects her things . . . jacket, keys, or some such.

Paige Where are you . . . What are you doing – ?

Nikki You don't need a doctor.

Paige . . . What?

Nikki Come on. I'll take you to a chemist.

SCENE SIX

Jo's office.

A large oil painting can be seen. It used to be an austere portrait of a woman but now has several large gashes.

Jo So the Principal of St Claire's called me this morning . . .

Gerald –

Jo You see, apparently . . . *apparently* . . . an 1892 portrait of their founding Principal disappeared from their dining hall last night. The current Principal called to ask if I wouldn't mind looking around my own college, and I assured her it wouldn't be here – of course it wouldn't be here! – but then I went downstairs to make a coffee, and oh . . . there she was . . . hanging up above the pancake machine.

Beat.

Gerald Okay. Firstly. Let me just say, we didn't mean to –

Jo There's a photo online, Gerald. Someone at St Claire's found it. You, Chris Poulton-Taylor, Aaron Beade and Tom Browning, in a bar, offering your drinks to one Miss Winifred May Heap – do not sit there and tell me you didn't steal this –

Gerald No, no, we definitely stole it –

Jo Okay then –

Gerald But we just wanted to take her out to a few bars, show her a good time, you know?

Jo Of course!

Gerald And after we took some pictures, we were going to put her right back, but we couldn't get in through the same door, so we had to climb over a fence, but it had barbed wire on the top, and she got kind of stuck, so we went back the other way, but it ripped even more . . . so . . .

Jo So what do you propose I do about this?

Gerald Um . . . don't you . . . you know . . . have a budget?

Jo A budget?

Gerald You know . . . to cover things like this?

Jo You know about that?

Gerald Two-hundred and fifty thousand? We have two hundred and fifty thousand pounds –

Jo That's not . . . that's not a target *to hit*. Every year, you don't get two hundred and fifty thousand pounds' worth of wanton destruction; it's a *contingency* –

Gerald For 'general wear and tear' –

Jo And what part of dragging an antique painting through a barbed wire fence constitutes that?

Gerald Well . . . it's definitely torn, so –

Jo Yes, that's a pretty accurate description, Gerald!

Gerald Okay . . . so . . . I guess we'll pay for it then.

Jo That is going to be an extraordinary amount of money.

Gerald We're going to split it.

Jo Ah, but you see, I still have a problem. St Claire's is probably expecting that payment to come with some kind of edification –

Gerald We are fee-paying students and cannot be forced to participate in rehabilitative labour programmes under any circumstances, nor can we be threatened with expulsion if we compensate the college in full for any damage caused outside the bounds of 'general wear and tear', as outlined in every student's signed terms of agreement.

Jo Who told you to say that?

Gerald No one.

Jo You just thought that up yourself, did you?

Gerald Yes.

Jo And how is Tom's dad these days? Still a lawyer, I'm assuming?

Silence.

Right. If you wouldn't mind sending Chris in to see me? Although I'm sure I'm about to hear the same speech . . .

Gerald Actually, can I just . . . can I talk to you about something?

Jo What?

Gerald The uh . . . the prayer room?

Jo's demeanour changes. She's excited . . . proud.

Jo Well . . . it hasn't been officially announced, but I can tell you it has been approved. We begin renovating next month –

Gerald I'm not going to use it.

Jo Sorry?

Gerald I just wanted to let you know that if you build a prayer room, I'm uh . . . I'm probably not going to use it.

Jo Aren't you . . . Sorry, aren't you Muslim?

Gerald I mean . . . kind of?

Jo Kind of?

Gerald I mean, I will be . . . eventually . . . but while I'm at university, I'm sort of on Muslim Rumspringa.

Jo Rumspringa.

Gerald Yeah.

Jo Like . . . the Amish kids, in . . . / in America –

Gerald In America, yeah –

Jo But the Muslim version –

Gerald *Exactly.*

Beat.

Jo Is that . . . common in . . . in Malaysian culture, or –

Gerald I'm hoping it could be? I mean, I've decided it could be, but if you build a prayer room and then you make me have my photo taken in front of it –

Jo But why would I make you –

Gerald Because you do it all the time. If you're taking a photo for the college website or whatever and you realise it's got a bunch of white people in it, you call me over –

Jo Well, sometimes I do, but –

Gerald And sometimes you ask me to put my arm around them, but like . . . I have no idea who these people are –

Jo Gerald, I'm sorry, I . . . I suppose I'm not really sure what you're asking me to do –

Gerald I'm not asking for anything, I – I don't need you to *do* anything – I just . . . I just want to experience this place like it is, like – like how it's been for hundreds and hundreds of years, and –

Nikki knocks and enters.

Nikki Hi, can I, um – (*Stops, sees Gerald.*) Sorry. I can come back or . . . (*Sensing, but not understanding, the tension in the room.*) Should I wait outside, or –

Jo Now isn't a good time, Nikki –

Gerald I don't have anything else I need to say, so –

Jo Yes, but –

Gerald Thank you for listening to me –

Jo Gerald –

Gerald I appreciate it, and I'm sorry about the . . .

He indicates the forgotten painting.

I'll get my dad to, uh –

Jo Thank you, that would be . . . I'll wait to hear from him.

He nods goodbye to her, exits. Jo is already exhausted.

Nikki . . . I wasn't expecting to see you so soon –

Nikki Yes, I know but –

Jo If you're here to interview me for your blog –

Nikki No –

Jo Maybe this can wait for another day – ?

Nikki What do I do if I'm aware a student at this college has been sexually assaulted?

Jo looks up. Now careful. Alert.

Jo By a student here?

Nikki Yes. A third year. He um . . . He went back to a fresher's room, she told me she passed out and um . . . he had sex with her anyway . . .

Jo (*getting out a pen*) What's the girl's name?

Nikki I . . . can't tell you.

Jo Why not?

Nikki She doesn't want anyone to know about it.

Jo Could you talk to her for me? Explain that I would be happy to talk this through with her –

Nikki She won't talk to you –

Jo Maybe she just needs some reassurance –

Nikki She doesn't know I'm here. She told me, um . . . she asked me not . . . not to tell anyone, but . . . I needed to . . . right?

Pause.

Jo So . . . this young woman . . . she doesn't want any involvement or assistance from the college.

Nikki No.

Jo Does she want to report it to the police?

Nikki No.

Jo Does she consider what happened to her to be an act of sexual assault?

Beat.

39

Nikki Well, no, but . . . I mean, she's clearly been assaulted, so –

Jo And there is a policy in place to deal with this, a key tenet of which is: I cannot action anything without this young woman's permission –

Nikki So you're going to ignore it – ?

Jo No. Of course I'm not, but . . . Look, it might be helpful for you to recognise . . . what one person considers an assault, another might consider an issue of – / I don't know –

Nikki What – ?

Jo Judgement.

Nikki Judgement –

Jo She's eighteen . . . yes? She's away from her parents for the first time. So she's going to drink, and she's going to have sex, and some of that sex, no doubt, she'll wake up to regret –

Nikki And you don't think the guys know that? You don't think they've maybe factored that kind of . . . I don't know . . . that kind of *vulnerability* into their plans –

Jo No. I don't. Having met most of them, I'm pretty sure that kind of scheming is a little beyond them –

Nikki There is a *culture* here –

Jo Oh no.

Nikki There is a culture of –

Jo No. No no no no no – Nikki, we are talking about one possible incident. *One.* You cannot take one possible incident and from that start extrapolating a *culture* –

Nikki One in five.

Jo One in five what – ?

Nikki One in five women are sexually assaulted while attending a university –

Jo And where did you get that statistic from – ?

Nikki Where – ?

Jo Yes. Where?

Nikki Like . . . like . . . *everywhere.*

Jo Everywhere –

Nikki Everyone knows it.

Silence.

Jo Do you understand what you're accusing this college of? No – I know you've probably read that phrase in some prescribed book of feminist theory, but do you actually know what it means when you put the word 'rape' in front of the word 'culture' –

Nikki Of course I –

Jo It means that that adjective captures the dominant attitude or behaviour of an *entire* society. Can you honestly say that women, at this college, overwhelmingly, and predominantly, are impacted by a culture of *rape*?

Nikki I don't know. Are they?

Jo Sorry?

Nikki Have there been others? Do you have records? Does the college document complaints – ?

Jo Nikki, you know I can't disclose that –

Nikki I'm a Student Representative, I'm a – I'm a Welfare Officer –

Jo Then you can help me by encouraging this young woman to see me, but if you're more interested in waging an ideological battle, / then I'm sorry, but –

Nikki But that's what it is! That's – that's *exactly* what it is. And you and I – we're supposed to be on the same side –

Jo And men on the other? Men need to be policed, right? Women, protected – I'm sorry, I've never bought into those kinds of distinctions –

Nikki But the article, you – you *marched* for it –

Jo No. I didn't. A nineteen-year-old student was raped and murdered while walking back from a night-time class – and the university? They suggested women stop taking night classes at all. Marching was an act of *power*, and – and defiance – I wasn't out there suggesting that all women should live in fear –

Nikki But that's what I *feel*, that's . . . Sometimes, that's *exactly* what I feel –

Jo And I'm not denying that you do. You obviously feel this – and – and *very* deeply – but the thing is, Nikki, I can't speak to your *feelings* on this – we have procedures in place to –

Nikki So it's me then.

Jo What?

Nikki I'm the problem.

Jo That's not what I said –

Nikki No no, it makes sense. I need to relax a bit. Develop a sense of humour, right?

Jo (*settling in, under her breath*) Ohh-kay –

Nikki It's what you told me last time, isn't it? And at first I thought . . . yeah . . . okay . . . maybe she's right . . . of course, of *course* it's me, but now . . . I dunno. Maybe it's you.

Jo Oh really?

Nikki Maybe – Maybe you can't see that there's a problem because you're actually part of the problem –

Jo Well Jesus Christ, Nikki, you could trap anyone with that argument –

Nikki WHY WON'T YOU TAKE ME SERIOUSLY?

Silence.

Jo Okay . . .

Jo turns, moves to her files, talking as she does so. During this, Nikki turns away, full of hot anger but also deep shame at having shown that level of emotion.

Okay, I'm going to give you a copy of our Misconduct Policy. I think the best thing you can do is to give this to the young woman so that she knows the proper avenues through which to make a complaint – if that is, in fact, what she would like to do –

Nikki I, uh . . . I think I need to go?

Jo Are you sure?

Nikki Yes. Um. I'm sorry, I . . . I didn't mean to raise my voice –

Jo It's okay. Don't worry about it. Listen, why don't you stay here for a while –

Nikki No, uh –

Jo I can make us both a cup of coffee, or – or a tea – ?

Nikki No – thank you –

Jo Because it seems like you might still be a bit upset –

Nikki I'm fine –

Jo Nikki –

Nikki enters a slightly different setting, though it shouldn't be immediately clear where she is. From the Voices, a gentle hum or murmuring . . .

Nikki opens her mouth, ready to broadcast into the void but –

SCENE EIGHT

The college laundry.

Paige What are you doing here?

Nikki What am I . . . ? It's a communal laundry, Paige –

Paige Then I'll come back later –

Nikki I didn't mention you. Not once.

Paige looks around, makes sure no one is in earshot, before –

Paige You said there was a rapist at college, Nikki –

Nikki I didn't say who it was –

Paige 'A fellow student.' 'A star athlete.' 'A university poster boy with his face on / an actual-fucking-poster.'

Nikki Twelve people read my blog. Twelve. And that's a *good* day. Mostly, I just use it as this giant empty void to practise writing my future opinion columns – I didn't think it would actually be *shared* –

Paige Have you seen how many times – ?!

Nikki Three hundred and seventy-four times. So far.

Paige *So far – ?*

Nikki And you want to know why? Because what happened to you happened to these women as well. Some

44

at this university. Some at this *exact* same college. One was a student here in 1998, another was here in 2019 – one woman – she was here last year – she thinks that *she* was the victim – she thinks I'm writing about *her* – people are talking about this, Paige, we can't let it go –

Paige *We* – ?

Nikki (*indicating Paige's laundry basket*) Are those the sheets?

   Beat.

If those are the bed sheets, then please *please* don't wash them –

Paige I can't sleep in dirty sheets –

Nikki I'll lend you some of mine –

Paige No – thank you –

Nikki We can go to the shops, right now, I'll buy you another set –

Paige I like these ones! From far away it just looks like a normal pattern, but then you get up close and you realise it's cats. Space cats. Tiny kitty-kat-astronauts floating around in deep celestial space – I didn't want something stupid with like – like daisies, or – or birds, or – or pink fucking polka dots, my mum and I went to three different shops, this is *exactly* what I was looking for, and . . .

   Beat.

Did the . . . Did Joma really say I had an issue with . . . with judgement?

Nikki Yeah. She also wanted to give you a copy of the Misconduct Policy, but you already have it, so –

Paige Do I – ?

Nikki Everyone does. It's in your Welcome Pack. Except I don't think anyone's ever actually read it –

45

Paige Except you. Right?

Nikki Yeah, but . . . Paige, I didn't read it for *fun*, I read it because –

Paige What does it say?

Beat.

Nikki Basically . . . you have two options. One. You're free to go to the police. Make this an external investigation. But then you'll have to submit to multiple examinations by police officers, an invasive hospital procedure to find evidence that's probably no longer there, and then a lengthy, exposing, possibly expensive legal process –

Paige What's the second option?

Nikki The college could conduct its own internal investigation.

Paige Okay . . .

Nikki Faster . . . lower burden of proof –

Paige That's good, right – ?

Nikki Yeah, except they'll have to set up a committee. Which will probably be run by people who don't believe this kind of thing happens here – people who have a vested interest in proving it doesn't – Tutors, Professors, Fellows – who, by the way, might not be an expert in this, might be – might be an expert in – in Maths or Geography or fucking Computer Science – all gathering to decide whether or not you're lying about something that happened in your own bed. And whether it's the college or the police who investigate this, it doesn't matter. Because the whole time, you'll be living in the same building as him, going to the same parties, sharing the same classes, eating in the same dining hall.

    Or . . . there's a third option. It doesn't involve the college. Or the police. But it does mean that things can be different now. Not in six months, or two years, or another generation – fucking *now* – but if the whole thing is going to work, it needs a real story at its centre –

Paige Nikki, I –

Nikki Yours. Maybe. Hopefully. Right now, we're in the middle of a groundswell, if it's going to turn into a fully fledged movement, then –

Paige *Movement* – what are you –

Nikki People are already connecting to this, Paige. They read your story; they see themselves; they feel brave enough to share – without it, there's no incentive –

Paige I don't want anything to do with this! I . . . I want it to go away, I . . . I got drunk, I was *stupid* –

Nikki Okay, and when it happened to me that's exactly what I thought.

Beat.

Paige When it . . . When has it happened to (you) – ?

Nikki So I get it, okay? I . . . I get it. Right now, all you want to do is pretend this whole thing never happened, but the thing is: it did happen. And it will happen again, and again and again and again, if not to you, then to some other girl –

Paige What happened to you, Nikki?

Silence.

Nikki –

Nikki If I tell you, I . . . I need you to understand . . . you'll be the first person I've ever told –

Paige Then you don't have to –

Nikki No. It's fair. You were brave enough to tell me yours.

Jo's office. Jo grasps an academic paper – triumphant.

Jo 'One in five'! 'One in five'! I found it. A 2007 study, of two American universities, which *claims* to be randomised, but for which participants *actually* self-selected. Worse, the questions conflate all unwanted sexual activity as assault: a stolen kiss, a drunken fumble, violent and forcible rape – all sitting together in the same problematic number . . .

Jo brings out more papers.

. . . One in four . . . One in ten . . . One in thirty-five . . . Six per cent . . . Thirteen per cent . . . this one . . . this one says sexual violence is now at an all-time low –

Leila But how does this –

Jo (*another paper*) Consent issues! Already prevalent in secondary school! Yet the first study would hold places of higher education *uniquely* responsible –

Leila Okay –

Jo (*another paper*) You want to know who faces more risk of sexual assault? Women who decide *not* to go to university!

Leila How long did you spend finding these?

Jo Not . . . not that long.

Leila A student came to you claiming sexual assault –

Jo Claiming a *culture* of sexual assault –

Leila And you're in here . . . what? You're checking her sources?

Jo Believe me, I would much rather spend this time speaking to the young woman in question, but if Nikki comes in here mapping constellations between unrelated events and unfounded statistics, then yes, I would like to be prepared –

Leila So why do you need me?

Jo I need a mediator.

Leila Right –

Jo No – she *requested* a mediator. And to be honest,
I wouldn't mind a bit of help keeping the conversation
on track.

Leila Does she know that we're friends?

Jo It doesn't have to be a secret.

Leila Is she aware that I have no experience in this sort of
thing –

Jo Leila, you're an esteemed and senior member of this
university community –

Leila She's not white, is she?

Beat.

Is she white?

Jo Sort of.

Leila Sort of?

Jo One parent, I suspect, is probably white –

Leila Oh . . . oh Josie –

Jo It's not like she's suffering from a lack of privilege,
Leila; she's a student here. *Here.* Before this, she went to an
elite private school – her mum's a GP, her dad's a clinical
psychologist – mine worked in a warehouse, my mother
scrubbed floors –

Leila I think you should find someone else –

Jo No, I – I want you, I . . . I *need* you. If I escalate this
myself or – or Nikki decides to go down the route of
a formal complaint – I could be tied up in twelve months

49

of bureaucratic nonsense, when all this requires is a . . .
a conversation.

You don't have to worry about her being outnumbered,
I asked her to bring the young woman with her – two of
them, two of us –

Leila This isn't a battle, Josie –

Jo I know, I know –

Leila We're not supposed to be preparing for combat –

Jo Spoken like a true mediator.

There's a knock at the door.

Please.
Please.
Please, Leila –

Leila Okay –

Jo Thank you –

Leila Can I just have a minute to –

Nikki appears.

Jo Nikki – hello – why are you by yourself?

Nikki I uh . . . I thought it might be better if . . . if you
talked to me first –

Jo And why is that?

Beat.

Nikki With respect, um . . . after our last conversation,
I didn't . . . I didn't feel particularly . . . heard –

Jo I don't know why that is –

Nikki Sorry, could I just –

Jo You had ample opportunity to speak, Nikki. You *chose*
to express your true feelings on an internet blog –

Leila (*extending her hand*) Hello. Nikki. My name is Leila. Dr Leila Bahrami.

Nikki (*taking it*) Hi.

Leila I'm a research scientist over at the Epidemiology Unit. Non-communicable diseases, mainly. Stroke, cancer, diabetes . . . that sort of thing –

Nikki Okay –

Leila Needless to say, I have zero experience in mediation –

Jo Leila –

Leila I also think it's important for you to know that Jo and I have been friends for thirty-eight years. If you don't feel comfortable with this, I understand, and I recommend that you reschedule this conversation until a more appropriate mediator is found. If, however, it helps to have someone here who understands Jo Mulligan's formidable capacity to bulldoze a conversation . . . then I will stay. Which would you prefer?

Pause.

Nikki You . . . I think.

Leila Okay.

Nikki Okay.

Jo (*rapid, arranging chairs*) Okay! Okay – does anyone need tea, coffee, water – no – no – okay. Could I start by asking . . . please . . . where is the young woman this incident involves, and why . . . isn't she here?

Pause. Leila encourages Nikki to 'go ahead'.

Nikki I um . . . I said she didn't have to come to this meeting if she didn't want to.

Jo And . . . I'm assuming she didn't want to?

Nikki She's already been assaulted, I guess she didn't feel like being questioned about it.

Jo So . . . if I have questions for her . . .

Nikki You can speak to me.

Jo And then?

Nikki And then I'll speak to her.

Beat.

Jo It's just . . . Sorry . . . this doesn't seem a very efficient way of having a conversation –

Leila Jo –

Jo Does she exist?

Leila Josie –   **Nikki** . . . What?

Jo I mean, that's what we're all skirting around here – does this young woman actually exist – ?

Nikki Of course she does –

Jo Is it you? Nikki . . . if it's you, you can tell me –

Leila (*to Nikki*) You don't have to disclose anything you don't want to –

Nikki It's not me –

Jo Are you sure –

Nikki It's not me.

Jo Okay. Then . . . with respect . . . would you mind explaining to me exactly how you're qualified to speak for her –

Nikki Excuse me – ?

Jo She's a first-year student . . . yes? So you've just met her. And something terrible may or may not have happened to this young woman, so she needs to speak to someone –

preferably someone with experience in this sort of thing – and then this situation needs to be investigated – both of those services, as a third-year student, you are not – to the best of my knowledge – equipped to provide.

Beat.

Leila Nikki, would you like to –

Nikki I have experience.

Jo As what – ?

Leila Jo – please –

Jo Are you a counsellor? A police officer –

Leila Nikki, if you want to speak to any of her points you may, but if you're feeling uncomfortable, please don't feel you have to say anything at all –

Nikki I . . . I shouldn't have to –

Leila You don't.　　　　**Jo** This is a conversation,
　　　　　　　　　　　　isn't it – ?

Nikki Yes, but you're . . . you're putting me in a position where I have to . . . In order to help you understand, I have to . . . I have to *disclose* my own experience –

Jo You had no problem disclosing someone else's –

Leila Okay, we're going to stop this conversation now –

Jo No – Leila – you don't understand –

Leila I understand that the point of a mediated conversation / is to allow two people to express their points of view and without interruption –

Jo A young woman was assaulted, Leila, and she told Nikki – *explicitly* – that she didn't want the matter further pursued – and what does Nikki do? She betrays the girl's trust, she pursues the matter anyway, and when she didn't

53

get the response she wanted from me, she took her concerns directly to the internet –

Nikki I was fourteen. When it happened to me.

Leila Nikki . . . No one here expects you to –

Nikki Fourteen. I didn't think it was rape at the time, because . . . because they only used their hands, and . . . and because they were my friends –

Leila Okay, maybe we should –

Nikki I'd known some of these boys since I was a baby, we – we had Maths together – Geography – we – we caught the same bus – I used to sneak out at night, hang out with them in the park, and – I was used to doing everything they did – so when one of them stole a bottle of vodka, every time they took a shot, I took one too. And then . . . then I couldn't walk that well, and I . . . I didn't want to get in trouble for drinking, so I asked them to . . . to lie to my mum, so that I could sleep over, and . . . I remember . . . I remember *thanking* them, and . . . the only reason I even know they undressed me, and – and put their hands on my body and their – their fingers inside of me – is because one of them got out their phone and took photos of it, so when you say, when you say, I don't have the *experience*, that I . . . that I might not understand what I mean when I put the word 'rape' anywhere near the word 'culture' . . . *I* am the proof. So is she. Do I have to prove it any more definitively than that?

Silence.

Leila Nikki . . . thank you. I understand that would have been difficult for you to –

Jo Yes. I think you do.

Leila (*to Nikki*) If you want to leave, you can –

Jo Don't coddle her, Leila. She doesn't want to be treated like a little girl; she wants to be treated like a grown woman, / and that means listening to a few ideas that may be uncomfortable for her –

Leila Josie, right now, you are the one acting like a child –

Jo (*furious*) She had her time to speak, Leila – now it's mine.

Beat.

I'm sorry that happened to you, Nikki, I . . . I really *really* am. But you cannot take isolated incidents, one of which did not even happen in this college, and then publicly hold this institution accountable for a rape culture that has *not* been proven to exist –

Nikki moves to leave.

No, Nikki, wait. Please. We need to sort this out –

Nikki I . . . I don't think I can, I . . . I think I need to go –

Jo And I . . . I'm not sure I can risk you leaving to write a blog about it –

Nikki I'm more articulate in my blog. In the moment, I can't . . . I can't always make things sound as – as powerful as you can – I mean, I come in here, and – I have a *stutter*, I – I don't have a stutter anywhere else –

Leila Say it to me. Whatever it is you want her to understand, Nikki, say it to me –

Nikki I . . .
I know you find me difficult, Jo, and . . . and demanding. I know you don't have a lot of time for arguments based on feelings, and . . . and 'big emotions', but . . . what you don't seem to realise is that the ability to hold both sides of an argument, it's brilliant in a college tutorial, but in the real world . . . it doesn't move anything forward.

You know what creates change? Activists. Zealots. Difficult, demanding people who see possibility and, and hope, where others only see the work and – okay – yeah – you really tend to piss a lot of people off when you refuse to back down from the idea that things could actually be better, and – and people really *really* don't like it when you keep talking despite the fact you've already been dismissed, and if you have the audacity to do this to a person who is older than you, who – who has more power over you – then you are basically guaranteed to be continually fucked over by them in tiny-barely-perceptible ways, but I'll do it anyway . . . Jo. I'll be difficult. And demanding. I'll keep talking because I happen to value things bigger than how much you enjoy my company – a terrible thing happened in this building, and I'm going to do something about it –

Jo And would that be with or without the victim's consent – ?

Nikki With. Actually.
 But if your concern is genuine, I . . . I appreciate it.

SCENE TEN

Paige appears. Broadcasts into the void. It all begins in a place of intense focus, then rapidly devolves . . . expands.

Paige (*an online video; reading*) 'Skirts lifted. Bra straps pulled and snapped. Camera phones held underneath chairs or the closed door of a cubicle. Comments made, quietly, as you try to walk through the narrow space they've left or hurled at you from the anonymous safety of a speeding car.
 'Every young woman knows what it's like to live in a culture that views her body, first and foremost, as an object of sexual gratification. This isn't unusual, or unexpected; it's a culture that begins with a joke, a gesture, a throwaway word or a game between friends, and it ends in an act of violence.'

56

(*In her own voice.*) By now many of you will have read this post . . . written by a student called Nicole Stewart.

Four days later, many of you are by now questioning whether the incident described even occurred.

I am here to tell you that it did.

My name is Paige Hutson.

And during my first night at college . . . I was sexually assaulted.

By a student called Aaron Beade.

My College Master believes that what happened to me is a rare and isolated incident. Worse, she believes that that there is a scale of rape and that what happened to me is a lower-ranking 'issue of judgement' and therefore not worthy of her attention.

But I know

We know

That that's not the case

If you have experienced sexual assault at this college, or another college, or anywhere associated with a university campus, then I encourage you to follow the link at the bottom of this video . . .

Nikki (*an online post or video*) In just over six hours, we've received seventy-five individual stories. Please bear with us as we try to read and verify each of these submissions, and please continue to add

Voices I know

I know I know I know

Two years ago

Six years ago

I've never told anyone this but

In high school

I was nine

In the comfort of my own home

In class

I haven't worn a skirt since

57

your experiences. We will, of course, anonymise your stories before posting them on the website for others to read . . .

Paige (*an online video*) Yeah, so . . . I've just woken up . . . crazy twenty-four hours, but the website has now received . . . (*Checking.*) okay . . . two hundred and fifty-one stories . . .

Nikki (*an online post or video*) . . . Two hundred and seventy-eight stories . . . I keep refreshing the college website and . . . nothing . . . radio silence –

Paige (*an online post*) Three hundred stories. No public statement. I don't know what I expected. Concern, maybe? Sympathy? Shared and uninhibited rage –

Nikki (*an online post or video*) Where are you, Jo? Are you watching this? Are you listening? Is this enough evidence yet? Or would you like us to disclose more?

When I was twelve

I thought he was my best friend

Here I want to show you something

We weren't, like, officially dating, but
    We were friends, we were good friends, but
    I still can't remember his name, but
        This happened to me
        Here I want to show you something
        Two years ago
        Two months ago
        Enough talk, no more excuses
        How many more need to suffer
        Seventeen years ago
        Last week
        Just the kind of behaviour we've come to expect
        Can't say I'm fucking surprised
        I can't believe this is still happening
        This happened to me
        Thirty-two years ago
        I know I know I know
I know I know I know
        I know I know I know
I know I know I know

And more and more and more and more –	I know I know I know I know I know I know –

Jo appears, and with her, the Voices die down . . . though perhaps not entirely . . .

Jo (*an internal email*) Dear students,

I want to address the existence of a website that aims to collect and amplify stories of sexual assault from university students worldwide. While the intention is admirable, the resulting online discussion now threatens to overshadow the original incident.

To date, I have extended multiple invitations to meet with the young woman most directly affected. Until this conversation takes place, please do not mistake my public silence on this issue as a lack of care. I will always protect your right to engage in open and critical discussions, even if the subject of criticism is myself. But I am unwilling to cross the line from transparency to public spectacle, especially if this action threatens the respect, dignity, safety and privacy of my students.

It pains me to have to state what should be self-evident but let there be no ambiguity: sexual violence is a deplorable act, antithetical to the values we uphold as a society and within our college community. Thankfully, there is no evidence to suggest it is culturally endemic here. At this moment, I strongly encourage each of you to review our Misconduct Policy –

Nikki (*a blog post*) At the end of my first year of university, I considered transferring to a different college. But I stayed. Because they hired Jo Mulligan. A self-professed feminist. A no-bullshit ex-broadcast-journalist who wears trainers to formal dinners, drinks with her students, and sometimes swears in her speeches. Jo Mulligan is the first female Master this building has ever had. And I wanted to know what it was like to live and study in a place like this when it's run by someone like her.

The answer is: . . . 'No different, really. It's exactly-the-fucking-same.'

Blackout.
    End of Act One.

Act Two

Nikki appears. Sings or recites the old British folk song 'The Cuckoo's Nest'.

Nikki
As I was a-walking one morning in May
I met a pretty fair maid and unto her did say:
'It's for love I am inclined, and I'll tell you me mind
That me inclination lies in your cuckoo's nest.'

'My darling, 'says she, 'I am innocent and young
And I scarcely can believe your false deluding tongue
Yet I see it in your eyes and it fills me with surprise
That your inclination lies in me cuckoo's nest.'

Some like a girl who is pretty in the face
And some like a girl who is slender in the waist,
But give me a girl that will wriggle and will twist,
At the bottom of the belly lies the cuckoo's nest.

Paige appears, contributes her voice.

Nikki *and* **Paige**
'Then my darling,' says he, 'if you see it in my eyes,
Then think of it as fondness and do not be surprised.
For I love you, my dear, and I'll marry you, I swear,
If you let me clap my hand on your cuckoo's nest.'

'My darling,' said she, 'I can do no such thing,
For my mother often told me it was committing sin
My maidenhead to lose and my sense to be abused,
So have no more to do with my cuckoo's nest.'

Some like a girl who is pretty in the face
And some like a girl who is slender in the waist,

But give me a girl that will wriggle and will twist,
At the bottom of the belly lies the cuckoo's nest.

Nikki and Paige begin to play havoc. They punch up the tempo, add beats, dance moves, etc., then fold in additional songs: fragments from university drinking songs, rugby songs, prison songs, bawdy ballads and sea shanties. A symphony of other Voices support them.

    Suggestions from real songs are listed below – additions and extractions welcome – but the sequence should layer, build, become surprising, perhaps staggering, in scope.

    Leila, towards the end, may enter and observe . . .

I wish that all the ladies
Were bells up in a tower
And if I was the bell boy
I'd bang them every hour

I wish that all the ladies
Were buns upon the shelf
And if I was the baker
I'd cream them all myself
(*etc.*)

—

Take off all your underwear
I don't care if you're there
Bye bye blackbird
You took me to your
   bungalow
in wildwood
There I took advantage
of your childhood
I took off your lovely dress
Looking for your blackbird's
   nest
Blackbird bye-bye

—

Oh let down your
   drawbridge
I'll enter your keep
Enter your keep nonny-nonny
Enter your keep nonny-nonny
Let down your drawbridge
I'll enter your keep

—

Four and twenty virgins
came down from Inverness
And when the ball was over
there was four and twenty
   less
Balls to your partner
arse against the wall
If you never get fucked
on a Saturday night
You'll never get fucked at
   all

—

62

Y-O-U-N-G, we like 'em
    young
Y is for your sister
O is for oh so tight
U is for underage
N is for no consent
G is for go to jail

—

The Mayor of Bayswater
has such a lovely daughter
And the hairs on her
    dicky-di-do
Hang down to her knees

One black one, one white one
and one with a bit of shite on
The hairs on her dicky-di-do
Hang down to her knees

—

All the nice girls love
    a candle
All the nice girls love a wick
Cos there's something about
    a candle
That reminds them of a –
(*Clap clap.*)

—

It was on the good ship
    Venus
By Christ you should have
    seen us
The figurehead was a whore
    in bed
Sucking on a penis

—

Up and up
Went the level of steam
Down and down
The level of cream
Till at last
The young girl cried . . .
'Enough, enough,
I'm satisfied.'
And now we come
To the tragic bit
There was no way
Of stopping it
And she was split
From arse to tit
The whole bloody lot
Was covered in shit

—

These are the girls that
    I love best
Many times I've sucked
    their breasts
Fuck her standing
Fuck her lying
If she had wings
I'd fuck her flying
Now she's dead but not
    forgotten
Dig her up and fuck her
    rotten

63

A small disused laboratory or university office.

Nikki Did you know?

Leila Know what? That this thing existed? Or that my husband wrote in it?

Nikki That he um . . . wrote in it –

Leila He's a Professor of Poetry; I imagine, as a student, he also had a passion for the subject –

Paige It's not really poetry though, is it –

Leila Isn't it?

Nikki It's a hymnal – see? The oldest entry is 1897, but it's been updated almost every year since – new songs – amendments to old ones –

Leila Then 'Michael Danfield, 1979' probably considered this task to be of the greatest historical importance . . .

Paige Yes, but . . . he's Chair of the College Board –

Leila In 1979 he was a student –

Nikki Who grew up to be Chair of the College Board –

Leila (*reading*) '"The Cuckoo's Nest". Traditional English folk song. Earliest written mention, late 1600s. The cuckoo is a recurring motif in English folklore, often symbolising themes of unfaithfulness. The "nest", in this instance, is a metaphor for a woman's genital area –' Does that sound like a young man interested in anything more than an academic approach?

Nikki Dr Bahrami, I . . . I understand if this is . . . kind of confronting for you, but –

Leila They're songs, Nikki. Just songs. You have four hundred and eighty-two examples of tangible sexual assault. If you start linking those stories to innocuous things like an English folk song, then you're just leaving your campaign open to easy criticism –

Paige We're already being criticised –

Leila Yes, I – I know –

Nikki (*re online comments*) 'Fuck you feminist fucks.'

Paige 'One drunk bitch can't keep her pants on and our whole college has to suffer –'

Leila That's abuse. Students, probably. Just worried there might now be a college-wide ban on alcohol – I'm talking about criticism from people with a serious following. Journalists, academics – *feminist* academics –

Paige Saying what – ?

Leila Paige, by the early 1990s, all the major legal battles in Western feminism had already been won –

Paige Um – okay – no –

Nikki Overt discrimination, maybe, but not inequality –

Paige (*listing*) Economic inequality, violence, social norms, attitudes –

Leila Yes, but I'm not talking about ideas or theories; I'm talking about objective political realities –

Paige / 'Objective political realities' – ?

Nikki What does that . . . What does that even *mean* –

Leila It means before 1975 a woman couldn't open a bank account in her own name. It means that rape within marriage wasn't recognised as a criminal offence until at least 1991 –

Nikki And what? You think your generation solved everything –

Leila Not everything. And not me, personally. But others, including the current Master of your college – they had a significant part in improving things. Not, they believed, for themselves, but for you. Josie is not someone you can accuse of laziness or complacency. Before either of you were even born, she was using her voice to speak up, and out, at significant risk to her own career, her own personal relationships, and if you stand in front of her, or women like her, and dismiss them out of hand – worse, try to sell them, instead, on your own 'new and improved' version of feminism –

Nikki And what exactly is our version of feminism – ?

Leila Honestly? I have no idea. It's confused. Inconsistent. Borderline schizophrenic –

Paige Whoa – okay –   **Nikki** Right – okay –

Leila No? You don't think so – ?

Paige No –   **Nikki** No, not really –

Leila You celebrate modern sex work as empowering while ignoring that for most women it's the result of trafficking or poverty or lack of alternatives –

Paige Um . . . okay –   **Nikki** Well . . . yeah, but –

Leila You go on slut walks to protect Western women from being judged for their revealing clothing, yet you accuse anyone of criticising the hijab as Islamophobic –

Paige No, I – I would   **Nikki** Okay, but . . .
never –   that's . . . that's not –

Leila When I was eleven years old, two of my cousins, both young men, boys, the age you are now, were jailed – beaten – publicly executed – for criticising the widespread removal of every right that women, in this country, your country, currently take for granted – even *now*, that fight continues – and you – with your freedom of movement, your freedom of education, your freedom of speech – all that freedom – you dare to protest a few hundred songs?

Beat.

Paige Dr Bahrami, I . . . I'm so sorry, I –

Nikki We're not unaware of our privilege, Dr Bahrami. I think it's important that we acknowledge it, but . . . things can change . . . right? An election can be lost or won. A global pandemic can break out. In an instant, everything a previous generation fought for can be reversed or – or erased – and what your family's story demonstrates, I think, is not the need for cynicism, but . . . but vigilance.

There's a brief flicker of something between Leila and Nikki, a new wariness that neither wants to voice. Paige remains oblivious.

Leila Good. *Good.*

Paige Wait . . . Was that . . . Was that a test – ?

Leila Consider it a practice run. Then it won't shock you when someone else says these things to you on a public panel –

Paige Right. Okay. Um . . . *thank you* –

Nikki Leila, I . . . I'm really sorry I have to push this, but –

Paige Nikki – don't –

Nikki Considering your connection to – to Professor Danfield and – and Jo Mulligan –

Paige Nikki –

Nikki We just want to be reassured, please, that anything we discuss with you won't be shared with –

Paige Oh my God, *Nikki* –

Leila I promise.

Beat.

You're not wrong, Nikki. What you've sensed, this . . . this intangible thing, this . . . 'culture'? It exists. I've experienced it. You've experienced it. Jo, absolutely, has experienced it, and I am appalled that the responsibility for educating everyone else, falls, once again, to young women, whose only concern, right now, should be on completing their university degrees, so . . . I'm here to help you. That help is there, if you want it, but –

Nikki I do.   **Paige** We do.

Leila Then this space is yours for as long as you need it. I've crossed it off the department calendar. (*Leaving.*) As long as you don't mind sharing your campaign headquarters with old lab benches and Bunsen burners – I'd give you all the time in the world if I could, but I have a PhD student who needs to discuss 'a bold new intervention in managing heart disease', so –

Paige Go – please –

Leila My office is down the hall. Let me know when four hundred and eighty-two stories become five hundred. You're my heroes. (*To Nikki.*) Both of you.

Leila exits. Paige blooms under the praise. Nikki is unsettled.

Paige We need to take the songs down.

Nikki What? No – why – ?

Paige Leila's right, we don't want to . . . to confuse or . . . I mean, they're just songs, they're stupid songs – I never should have suggested it –

Nikki The videos are fantastic. It was a brilliant idea, Paige – they're going viral, they're bringing this whole new audience to the website –

Paige But Leila said –

Nikki So what? She has useful insight, free office space she can delegate at her will, but . . . we can't forget who's really running this campaign –

Paige You?

Beat.

Nikki Us. You . . . you know I was going to say us, right – ?

Paige Hey – I'm joking! Joking. I know it's ours. I only built the entire website –

Nikki And it's fucking magnificent –

Paige I know.

They grin at each other – an easy silence.

You're really good at this. You know that, don't you?

Nikki Good at what – ?

Paige I don't know how you just . . . start talking and then . . . and then make it sound . . . *good* –

Nikki Yeah, well, it doesn't always so –

Paige You should be the one doing all the talking. Not me.

Nikki It's your story –

Paige You have a story too –

Nikki Yeah, and it's on the website –

Paige Anonymously –

Nikki We made all the stories anonymous –

Paige But yours doesn't have to be? You and I, we could . . . We could do this together. We could . . . We could both be the face of this . . . this thing, this . . . this movement, *together*, and –

Tamara enters, Gerald trailing somewhere behind . . .
deeply uncomfortable.

Tamara Paige?

Beat.

Are you Paige Hutson?

Paige . . . Who are you?   **Nikki** . . . Ghazali, what are
                                   you – ?

Tamara My name is Tamara.

Paige Tamara . . . ?

Tamara Tamara Beade. Aaron's mother. I want to talk to
you –

Nikki No . . . No, you shouldn't be here –

Tamara Nikki . . . right? Nikki, I . . . I just thought if Paige
and I could have a conversation, then maybe we could
reach some kind of resolution –

Paige Nikki, what is going on? / Gerry, I . . . What is this?

Nikki I – I don't know, I –

Tamara Paige, I don't claim to understand / what happened
between you / and my son –

Nikki Do you actually think this is okay, Ghazali – ?!

Paige Just leave it, Nikki – let's go –

Tamara But I'm not sure it's worth destroying someone's
life over?

Beat. Paige falters, turns.

Nikki Paige . . .

Paige Maybe . . . (*Bolsters her own courage.*) Maybe your
son should have thought about that before he –

Tamara But he didn't, did he? He can barely remember it – neither can you. So if you decide to go to the police with this, it's not even 'he said – she said', it's your lack of memory versus the total abyss of my son's –

Paige Okay, but this . . . this happens all the time . . . right, Nikki? This happens all the time to women, and . . . and maybe . . . maybe if someone actually goes to jail for it – ?

Tamara NOT my son. (*Looking around, lowering her voice but not her intensity.*) *Not* my son. He's not some sacrifice for your schoolgirl activism, Paige – he is a twenty-one-year-old *kid* –

Nikki Paige, please, you don't have to listen to this –

Tamara And you, you're so . . . Paige, you're so young. Hiding behind that screen, you think you can say whatever you want to, but the blog posts, the comments, the – the videos, the website, that is *forever* . . . do you understand that? People will look you up, and they will find him, and people will look him up, and they will find you . . . forever.
Please . . . please . . .
Whatever it is you think you're doing just . . . stop.

Silence.

Thank you, Paige. I appreciate your time.

Beat.

Gerald . . . if you wouldn't mind showing me the way back?

Jo's office.

Michael Five hundred. Five hundred and ten stories –

Jo From across the country. No parameters around time. Or place. No attempt to define what sexual assault *actually* means. So the only thing those stories currently prove is that isolated incidents *do* happen –

Michael But when you're reading them, the . . . the fear, as . . . as a parent –

Jo You mean, as a potential fee-paying parent –

Michael I mean as a father. The fear that your child might be harmed, it's . . . it's animal. No parent would send their child to a place where there is even a hint of this, so . . . a public statement, maybe –

Jo I've already written an email – sent it to every student and staff member –

Michael Jo –

Jo And I stand by what I said: no one should be engaging with this until I've had a chance to speak to this girl, but short of going to her door and knocking on it, Paige Hutson, currently, is ignoring every email –

Michael Because right now she's busy having a conversation directly with the internet –

Jo And your wife, I'm told, is helping them to do it.

Beat.

Michael I . . . Jo, if possible, I'd like us to try and keep this separate, please –

Jo Separate? Michael, you share a bed with their campaign advisor; how do I know this conversation isn't being ferried straight back to headquarters?

Michael Because she won't talk to me. Leila told me explicitly – stay out of it. I'm the enemy too, you see – Chair of this organisation, friend to you – and it's not making home life particularly pleasant, so if you've said something to offend her, Jo –

Jo *Me – ?*

Michael Please. Fifteen years I've been on the Board, she rarely attends a function – you become the Master, she's out there providing safe refuge to our students –

Jo (*reading an article*) 'This isn't your typical hymnal, but a college joke dating back to roughly 1875. Among the hundreds of contributors is none other than the current Chairperson, Professor Michael Danfield –'

Michael Oh my God –

Jo '– penned during his days as a student in 1979.'

Michael Who wrote that – ?

Jo Student newspaper – don't worry, it gets worse. 'The uncovering of this songbook is the latest in a series of controversies that have long beset the institution. In 1986, the body of university student, Alison Welsh –'

Michael *Alison Welsh – ?*

Jo '– was found less than one hundred metres from the college grounds –'

Michael In 1986! 1986!

Jo 'To date, no individual has been brought to justice or charged.'

Michael But every single member of this community was *cleared*. I'd already left by then – I was lecturing at Sheffield, for Christ's sake. And yet every time there's a hint of controversy – *every time!* – some student journalist brings it up again as if it's all intricately related. You do not sing a song, then go out and *murder* a woman –

Jo No, you just like to clap your hand on her cuckoo's nest –

Michael I was twenty-one. Twenty-one years old. Are the contents of my entire life to be dragged out and – and *rummaged* through –

Jo I don't think she had to search all that hard; Nikki probably found it in the college library –

Michael Which is exactly where it belongs! Collecting those kinds of drinking songs, it was . . . it was supposed to be –

Jo Of the greatest historical importance – ?

Michael This isn't a joke, Josie –

Jo I know –

Michael This place is my work, my – my life – my reputation –

Jo And this is exactly how they want you to react. So don't. You're right. This is crude sensationalism – disrespectful to Alison. And the best thing we can do is refuse to play into this kind of lazy journalism –

Michael And that's it, is it?

Jo Yes. That's it.

   Beat.

Michael Could I just ask . . . would making some . . . some perfunctory show of support be such a bad thing?

Jo Depends. What would the show involve?

Michael / A public statement . . .

Jo 'A public statement' . . .

Michael You could . . . I don't know . . . *acknowledge* these young women and their . . . their bravery –

Jo Their / *bravery* – ?

Michael Their bravery in creating this . . . this 'inspiring' campaign –

Jo And if I don't think we should –

Michael Then this stops being a suggestion.

Beat.

Jo Need I remind you, Michael, I'm not the only one being shot at here –

Michael Well I certainly didn't start it –

Jo But you did! You all did! And I inherited it! I have been here for just over a year. I haven't even opened that . . . that *bloody* prayer room. I am going to transform this anachronistic lump of a building, but to do that, I need *time*. I need time to work out exactly what is going on here, *exactly* what this building is going to be, and I need you, Michael, as the Chair of my Board, to stand by me while I make that happen –

Michael And I will. It's just a statement. Something to . . . to douse the fire a bit – placate the rest of the Board in the process –

Jo I can't, I . . . I can't write something I don't believe –

Michael If you don't want to call them 'brave' – fine. Stick to the facts. Acknowledge their . . . their 'commitment to raising awareness' –

Jo You mean their flagrant disregard for the due process of law –

Michael My GOD, Josie – *please* – do *not* put me in a position where I have to fire you.

Beat.

Jo Is that . . . Why is that something that would even be considered?

Beat.

Michael?

Michael When you were hired . . . concerns were raised –

Jo Concerns –

Michael There were members of the Board who worried you might not . . . might not be the best fit for this organisation –

Jo Really –

Michael And I put myself on the line for you, Jo, I . . . I made an argument that – that in this increasingly difficult climate, we might benefit from someone who . . . someone who might help us to navigate difficult situations –

Jo I'm sorry, *what* –

Michael Please, Josie, this kind of thing is hardly outside the bounds of your professional interests –

Jo I'm a – a *journalist* – a – a correspondent, a presenter –

Michael The Master of a College needs to have some understanding – to – / to help us to – to navigate this –

Jo Oh no – no they don't. Your previous Master? He was a classicist with a side interest in large-scale garden mazes! The one before that? A Doctor of Theology – !

Michael There were certain expectations around your appointment – it's not sexism to recognise that your . . . your gender . . . it might naturally facilitate a closer connection with the young women at this college –

Jo Then I'm sorry to disappoint you, Michael, but being born with lady bits doesn't grant you entry to some homogenous cult of female-woman-people. We don't all think the same, act the same – some of us . . . some of us don't even *like* each other.

Michael Yes, Josie. That seems abundantly obvious now.

  Beat.

Jo You're scared. You're all scared, aren't you? If you don't get these girls on side, they'll keep digging. Christ, who knows what they'll find –

Michael I'm trying to *help* you –

Jo So perhaps you should go to the Board and divulge everything now.

Beat.

Michael I don't . . . Sorry, I don't think I understand –

Jo Come on, Michael. I wasn't the only student you ever slept with.

He laughs, shocked.

Michael Josie, that was . . . that was *consensual* –

Jo You were my lecturer –

Michael *Assistant* lecturer –

Jo You taught a class; you marked my papers –

Michael For one subject – that's it –

Jo Yes, and you also liked me to keep my shoes on while we –

Tamara Hi.

Tamara enters.

Sorry.
    I know it's rude to interrupt, but . . . to be honest, it's also slightly disrespectful to make me wait three-quarters of an hour –

Michael Sorry, you are –

Tamara Well, I was Dr Mulligan's twelve p.m. appointment, but it's now twelve forty-five –

Jo Mrs Beade, I am so sorry –

Michael Mrs Beade. I didn't realise you had a meeting with the college today –

Tamara With Dr Mulligan –

Jo (*coming forward to shake her hand*) Jo –

Tamara Call me Tamara – please –

Michael Tamara. I'm Professor Michael Danfield, Chair of the Board –

Tamara We've actually met a few times –

Michael Of course.

    Beat.

Tamara, if you'd like me to stay –

Tamara No, we'll be fine, thank you –

Michael I'd be more than happy to –

Tamara No.   **Jo** No.

    Silence.

Michael Jo, I . . .

    Silence.

I'll speak to you later.

    Michael exits.

Tamara In trouble, are you?

Jo . . . What makes you say that – ?

Tamara Don't worry. I couldn't make out anything of note. Look at these walls. The place is a fucking fortress. I've always thought so . . .

Jo Were you –

Tamara Oh. No. No. I was never clever enough to get in here. I went to the pleb university fifteen kilometres down the road. Still . . . it was close enough that I was able to accept one or two invitations . . .

She smiles, then realises that Jo doesn't.

We're not one of those families who send generation after generation of boys here – I hope you know that. Aaron worked hard – he picked this place himself –

Jo I imagine you want to talk about his suspension.

Tamara Among other things.

Jo I hope you understand . . . once that accusation was placed online –

Tamara Relax, Jo. I'm not here to attack you. Second only to my son, those girls have decided you're the villain here, so I'm hoping we might be able to help each other out . . .

Tamara removes a folder from her handbag – carefully tabbed and filed – but as she does, the papers slide out – drop – scatter all over the floor . . .

No! *Shit – no* – no no no no no –

Jo Here – it's okay –

Tamara No it's not okay – it's not . . . this – all of this, I . . . I haven't slept for thirty-six hours, I . . . I downloaded, printed, everything I could find – I was only just starting to make sense of it, the . . . God . . . look how much there is . . . the 'alleged victim', she . . . She's been somewhat exhaustive in her campaign.

Jo (*picking up the papers*) I think her target might be a little bigger than Aaron himself.

Tamara 'Skirts lifted . . . Bra straps pulled and snapped . . .'

Jo Yes –

Tamara A rape culture – 'an historical continuum of violence'.

Jo . . . Yes –

Tamara Except my son has been singled out to atone for it. And I don't think that's fair . . . do you?

Beat.

Jo Lucky kid.

Tamara Sorry?

Jo Having this kind of expertise on his side –

Tamara Oh, you think I'm . . . Really? You think I'm a lawyer –

Jo Are you?

Tamara I run a recruitment agency. My husband is in finance. Everything I know about this, I learned in the last five days . . .

Tamara finds a few pages, hands them over.

Here, this, in particular, is what I wanted you to read –

Jo Sorry, these are –

Tamara Forums. Online. Mothers of accused boys. All with stories – *all* the same. It's like . . . it's like the young women are going to parties – they're drinking alcohol – they're having some – some *terrible* sex – and one week, one month, half a decade later – something, someone politicises them – so they go back. They start to rewrite the narrative. It's a cultural phenomenon, all right – but it's not the one those girls think it is. And maybe . . . maybe if someone said something about it . . . Someone . . . someone with your standing –

Jo Oh . . . Oh, I'm not sure I have much of that –

Tamara I looked you up, Jo. I know exactly the kind of work you used to do –

Jo Tamara, I . . . To be honest with you, I . . . I'm starting to realise no one is particularly interested in what I might have to say about all this –

Tamara I know plenty. I have friends who are too scared to send their boys to a co-ed school. One friend . . . she told me she's sending her kid to college next year with a backpack full of consent forms –

Jo I . . . I'm head of this college. I have a duty of care to both students – I can't be seen to come out in support of either side –

Tamara And who does Aaron have on his side? Who? His study has been interrupted; his training has been suspended – he's supposed to be competing in a National Championship this year – the kid's fucking traumatised. My husband couldn't be here today because we're scared to leave Aaron alone, and . . . and I'm not sure what I'm supposed to say to my child, because currently, currently the best outcome we can hope for is that for the rest of his life he will only be *casually* referred to as a rapist instead of legally convicted as one.

Jo, I . . . I have a daughter too, I . . . I remember what it was like to be a young woman, I worry for her, but . . . I worry about the boys more. I have another son, a younger son. I now need to sit down, with a fourteen-year-old kid, and explain to him, that if he ever finds himself alone with a young woman, and that young woman has drunk herself *stupid,* then he needs to turn around, and he needs to get out of there as fast as he possibly can –

Jo I'm sorry, you're . . .

Beat.

No, sorry –

Tamara No, go on –

Jo You're telling your sons that if a young woman passes out in front of them, you'd like them to turn around, and . . . what? *Leave* –

Tamara Well what would you suggest – ?

Jo Sorry, I . . . I shouldn't even –

Tamara No – please –

Jo A blanket, maybe?

Tamara (*confused*) A blanket – ?

Jo A pillow under her head, a glass of water, check if – check if she's *breathing*, or . . .

> *Tamara starts laughing or crying, it's impossible to tell which.*

What's so funny?

Tamara A glass of . . . Of course! A glass of water, a blanket, a fucking *pillow* –

Jo Out of personal interest, have you . . . Have you ever talked with your sons about consent?

Tamara Have I ever – ?

Jo Have you ever had a conversation with your sons about the need for consent before putting *anything* inside of a woman's body –

Tamara And what? If I'd had that conversation with Aaron, none of this would have happened?
He's a good kid, Jo. Thirteen years of school, that child never received so much as a warning, and then . . . he came here.

> *She opens her file again, pulls out an events schedule.*

The 'tight and bright' party, the 'anything but clothes' party, the 'traffic light' party, drinking songs, drinking games, drinking competitions, 'What were you wearing when the police raided the brothel?' – should I go on?

If my son did anything *close* to what this girl describes . . . ?

It didn't happen under my roof. It happened under yours.

SCENE FOUR

Nikki's college bedroom.
Nikki has removed a few items of clothing from her wardrobe. Paige is holding a few of her own outfits.

Nikki Okay, so, I have this, or . . . Sometimes, I wear this with uh . . . this, and . . . actually, it would maybe go with that top you already have –

Paige Shouldn't I wear something . . . I don't know . . . more serious, or . . . or less colourful, or . . .

Nikki Actually, I uh . . . I kind of looked up articles of all the other students who have done this kind of thing, and . . . Look, there's no politically correct way to say this, but it's pretty fucking clear that the more beautiful you look in your photo, the more editorial space you get, so –

Paige Right – okay –

Nikki But don't worry. Let's find something that still makes you look and feel like yourself –

Paige (*spotting a shopping bag*) What's that?

Nikki Oh, um . . .

Paige You didn't buy me new clothes, did you?

Nikki No, of course not, it's just . . . I was in the shop anyway, and um . . .

She pulls out a new duvet cover, some new sheets – a set.

They don't have flowers or polka dots on them . . . at least?

Paige stares at the sheets . . . hugs her clothes to her chest.

Come on, Paige, it's . . . it's morbid. You're sleeping in the same sheets that . . . And look, I also think we need to ask the college for a new room, I mean it's kind of shocking they haven't offered to move you already –

Paige I called my mum this morning. To uh . . . To warn her about the article, and . . . Long story short, she's driving over, just . . . just as soon as she can get off work, so she might actually be here in a few days, or . . . or at the end of the week, or –

Nikki To . . . to help support you . . . or . . . Paige?

Paige You know I haven't made any friends here except for you?

Nikki Give it time. You definitely will –

Paige No one sits next to me in the dining hall. People stare at me when I walk across the courtyard. Yesterday, I went to my tutorial, I closed the door behind me, and my professor, he got right up and opened the door again –

Nikki So what? What does it matter about some stupid professor – Paige, a national newspaper wants to interview you! They're sending a photographer – this isn't some tiny write-up, okay – this is a feature article – and Leila's getting all these other requests – there's a magazine that wants to include you in a list – let me find the email, it's like –

Paige 'Fifteen young people who are going to change the world.' So far they've found a Rohingya refugee, a professional surfer whose leg was eaten by a shark, a climate activist . . . and me.

84

Nikki Paige, I . . . I don't understand what –

Paige I wasn't a virgin, by the way? I'd had sex. Last year. Once, and . . . I've done stuff with like . . . with two other guys, so –

Nikki That's not . . . It's not relevant –

Paige It was enough to be called a slut by some of the girls I went to school with, and Aaron's mum – she could find them online – she could contact them, and –

Nikki This is bigger than school, Paige. This is . . . This is bigger than college even – there's a whole community out there – women – men – we've just had our fifth story from a man, and – and every single one of them is a survivor, just like us –

Paige I hate that word, I . . . What did I survive, Nikki? Not a massacre. Not a . . . not a fucking shark attack –

Nikki You survived a (rape) –

Paige I hate that word more. It's not . . . It doesn't . . . Why isn't there another word for what happened to me –

Nikki Okay and when it happened to me I didn't want to use that word either, but . . . Paige I don't want you to look back in – in two years or – or three years – or five years – like I did! – and think . . . I *wish* I'd done something about it –

Paige Or maybe I wouldn't have thought about it at all.

Beat.

Nikki Are you going to leave the campaign?

Beat.

Paige Shit – Nikki, do you – do you realise how fucked up this is? I didn't realise until my mum made me see, but . . . I am *terrified* to disappoint you, like . . . I don't know how to explain to you exactly how much I *don't* want to speak to that journalist, but Mum said to me friends are supposed to feel safe enough with each other to say anything – even the hard stuff, and . . . I mean . . . We're friends . . . aren't we?

Nikki Of course we're friends –

Paige Okay. Good.

Nikki It's just . . . We connected because we'd both been assaulted –

Paige No . . . No that's not why I –

Nikki We became friends *because* of the campaign –

Paige So why am I the only one who's the face of it?

Beat.

Nikki My story is on the website too –

Paige Not your face. Not your name. And I keep wanting to share this space with you, and . . . Nikki, it doesn't make any sense to me, because between the two of us, you're the one who actually wants to be famous, so –

Nikki I want to be a journalist. I want to report from war zones, and – and interview Prime Ministers, and host panel debates, and, and documentaries and . . . I want to present the news, I don't want to *be* the news –

Paige And you think I do?

Nikki (*without break*) It's already an uphill battle for me, okay, because I don't get to walk into those spaces, with this face, and be treated as some neutral objective voice –

Paige Great – / okay – we're going there –

Nikki The assumption will always *always* be made that every time I open my mouth I have some personal political agenda –

Paige Please *please* don't make this about –

Nikki I can't make this more comfortable for you, Paige – the world is fucking unfair – and you can have some part

86

in changing the way things are and always have been – or you can leave, and – and go home to your mum, and – and whatever tiny little village you're from, and –

Paige And if I do that, we won't be friends any more –

Nikki Because I cannot *conceive* of doing nothing! I . . . I cannot *comprehend* how anyone could read six hundred and something stories, and just . . . just ignore them . . . worse . . . *abandon them*. Those women shared their stories because you promised them they were going to be heard, that things were going to change, and –

Paige So do the interview.
Do the interview, Nikki.
Find a fun colourful outfit that makes you look strong and smart and beautiful, but also young and straight and sexually inexperienced and mentally stable, and stand in front of a big ivy-covered wall, or . . . or sit on these boring fucking bed sheets, and have your photo taken in a national newspaper.
With me.

A long silence.

For what it's worth, Nikki, I . . . I didn't want to be friends with you because you'd been assaulted, I . . . I wanted to be friends with you because I thought you were *amazing* –

Nikki I'm sorry I disappointed you.

Beat.

Paige I'm sorry too, I . . . I'm sorry.

The college chapel.
  Gerald, alone . . . praying.
  Michael appears.

Michael What are you . . . *Stop* . . . Stop that –

Gerald stands up. At the same time, Michael spots the
prayer mat in his hands.

Gerald (*leaving*) Sorry, I . . . I didn't mean to, / I . . . I get
this probably isn't allowed, but . . .

Michael No . . . *no* – sorry – (*Quoting.*) 'I am in love
with every church and mosque and temple and . . .' Hafiz.
Muslim poet. Well, not Muslim exactly – no – Muslim –
Sufism is an ancient branch of Islam, it's just . . . (*Noticing*
Gerald's distress.) Is everything alright –

Gerald (*trying to leave*) It's fine – I can use my room, so –

Michael A lot going on here at the moment. All these . . .
revelations . . . pouring in. I imagine it must be . . .
confusing for you and . . . confronting? Women, they uh . . .
they tend to talk to each other, always talking . . . talking
talking talking, and men, we tend to . . . not . . . and . . .
What I mean to say is, it can be difficult to place yourself in
all this as a man, as a . . . as a *young* man, and –

Gerald I'm not upset about the campaign. I mean I am,
but . . . I'm kind of . . . I'm kind of finding it hard to think
about anything else right now except this . . . this one thing,
this . . . this person, and –

Michael Ah. And by person . . . you mean a young woman.

Gerald –

Michael A young man – ?

Gerald A woman –

Michael A woman, okay. And . . . you like her – ?

Gerald She's uh . . . It's complicated, and um . . . difficult, and . . . I don't really know how to . . .

Michael How to . . .

Gerald (*trying to leave again*) It's not a big deal, it's . . . I'm fine – it's nothing –

Michael I have to admit, I don't . . . I don't really know a lot about this sort of thing. When I was your age, women were sort of . . . a shadowy concept, and then . . . then I was lucky enough to meet my wife . . . here, actually, and . . . there's a . . . there's a sort of 'colouring in' that happens, when you fall in love, and, and then you have daughters – two of them – and my God, women become . . . *vibrant* and . . . and *detailed*, and . . . and it can be quite confronting to realise all the little ways you used to . . . What I mean to say is, the greatest relationships of my life, the most fulfilling wondrous people I know . . . all women. Complicated *difficult* women, and –

Gerald What if you had to choose though? What if . . . What if back then you had to choose between the friends you made here and –

Michael I'd choose her. Over and over again . . . I'd choose her.

   That's the strange thing about these sorts of places. I suppose we want you to choose us. So we sell you an idea – a prodigious one. We tell you all, 'These will be the best years of your life,' and we wrap it up in some ivy-clad fourteenth-century stone so it takes on the appearance of truth, but . . . how sad if it was true?

   For me, thankfully, the best years of my life, they're still happening. And I promise you, that has very little to do with the friends that I made here, and everything to do with the woman I fell in love with.

   Also . . . poetry.

Gerald Poetry?

Michael If you don't know what to say to this young lady, in my experience, it's always best to let someone else do it for you. Someone Persian, ideally –

Gerald Persian –

Michael Forugh Farrokhzad. For love. For all the ways love can hurt, and trap, and, and thrill, and . . . sustain. Farrokhzad. Trust me. English poetry is tasteless compared to it.

Gerald I uh . . . I might actually go look him up right now –

Michael Her –

Gerald Her – sorry – sorry . . . *her*, and um . . . Thank you . . . um . . . I think?

Michael You're welcome. Good luck.

Gerald exits.
Leila appears.

Leila You used to prescribe poetry to me. You had a poem for every ailment. Wordsworth for disconnection, Neruda for sorrow –

Michael Or joy –

Leila Mary Oliver for profound bouts of nihilism –

Michael How much did you hear?

Leila 'When I was your age, women were sort of . . . a shadowy concept.'

Michael Right.

Leila I was waiting by the car. You promised me a lift home?

Michael I'm sorry, I forgot –

Leila That's okay –

Michael Let me go get my things –

Leila Is anyone using the chapel tonight?

Michael I don't know.

Leila Can you maybe . . . check?

Michael Why?

Leila Because if no one is using it, Michael, I thought maybe we could fuck here.

Beat.

If you're worried about being discovered, you could keep your clothes on; I'll do most of the work –

Michael Leila, we need to talk –

Leila No, we're always talking – women – 'talking talking talking' – what I want – right now – is to fuck –

Michael I need to talk to you about Jo –

Leila No, I definitely don't want to do that –

Michael Leila. Please.

SCENE SIX

Jo, in the privacy of her college apartment.
    She observes (or is aware of) a growing multitude of Voices . . . comments, discussions, stories from student-victims of sexual assault, stories from mothers of accused boys, perhaps impossible to tell the difference . . .
Tamara may be somewhere in the mix. But also . . .
there is some burgeoning gossip around Jo and Michael's relationship . . . for example . . .

Voices (*forum posts/comments/videos/stories*) I watched, helplessly, as my son was wrongfully accused / One incident, one solitary incident / This happened to me / It was exaggerated, completely out of context / Two years ago / Five years ago / He actually considered that woman a friend / The threats / The death threats / How do I keep him safe? / Just wanted share this email / It was forwarded on / in confidence but / Have you seen this? / An email to the Board / It was sent to the Board / To all College Fellows / Did you know about this? / Have you seen this? / Here, I want to show you something . . .

Michael appears.

Michael (*an email*) Dear Josephine Mulligan,

You will have received, by now, an invitation to attend a meeting tomorrow, which concerns your ongoing position at this college.

Given the sensitive nature of this conversation and recognising a need for a fair and unbiased evaluation of the circumstances, I have informed the Deputy Chair about our past relationship. Following his advice, I am extending this disclosure to the wider Board; they will be apprised of this matter through a copy of this email.

Reflecting on our historical connection, I acknowledge that relationships between individuals in differing positions of authority, regardless of the era or mutual consent, necessitate careful consideration and, often, introspection.

Although policies in 1986 did not explicitly address such situations, I now understand the complexities involved and regret any actions on my part that may not have fully recognised these dynamics.

Please direct all further queries and communications to the Deputy Chair, who will be available to assist you during this period.

Kind regards,
Professor Michael Danfield.

At this, Jo decides to add her voice. As soon as she steps into the fray . . . the Voices die down to a gentle hum . . .

Jo Dear Members of the Board,

Thank you for the invitation to meet, and for your concern regarding my ongoing position. I, too, have concerns, and, sharing your desire for a fair and unbiased evaluation of circumstances, I have decided a meeting is unnecessary. I will share my concerns with you now.

While the Masters of yore were allowed to dick-jerk their way through long tenures with limited scrutiny, I, the first female Master, seem to be navigating a chapter of history marked by public shaming, haphazard data-gathering, and the repression of differing views.

It would be easy to blame this recent cultural shift on a few fervent student activists, but we must be honest with ourselves and recognise that they are only regurgitating the intellectually-barren-morally-questionable-bullshit, that you, as university scholars, have insisted on feeding them.

To illustrate the depths of this intellectual swamp, I took it upon myself to conduct an experiment this past month, crafting research papers under the nom de plume 'Dr Evelyn Whitestone', a name offered by a creative writing chatbot when I typed in the question, 'What is a good name for a fake Professor of Gender and Cultural Studies?'

Despite the fact that all of Evelyn's work is built on widely quoted unfounded statistics, as well as the dangerous assumption that rape culture can be found in benign spaces such as children's television programmes, indoor plant shopping, professional magic shows, natural land art and competitive dog grooming, four out of five of Dr Evelyn Whitestone's papers have so far been accepted for publication.

Rape is a vile, wretched, abominable crime. Yet we seem incapable of understanding complex and alcohol-fuelled interactions between young adults as anything other than evidence of its pervasiveness. This path we tread not only risks undermining the weight of this word, it also threatens to silence victims of genuine terror and violence, many of whom – surprise surprise – do not belong to the privileged circles of students that dominate this building.

Early on, I harboured a sincere wish to avoid all this noise and speak directly to the young woman involved.

I wanted to support her in sitting across from this
young man and saying the important words, 'You have
harmed me.' I wanted to help the young man, in turn, to
communicate his remorse and to accept his accountability.

Sadly, it is the young woman herself who has set the
terms of this conversation. She has demanded a trial by
public, and though I am grieved by her choice to remain
barricaded behind a social media campaign . . . I must
accept her decision.

Therefore, and with deep reluctance . . . you self-satisfied,
sanctimonious, chapel-fucking smut-singing professional-
poncho-wearing little-book-weevils . . . this is an open letter.

SCENE SEVEN

Paige's college room.

Gerald I saw the boxes in the hallway.

I guess I uh . . . I guess I just wanted to see if you were
alright, and . . . and I also really wanted to say sorry, for –

Paige I'm actually really busy right now, so –

Gerald She's his mum, okay? It's uh . . . It's really hard to
say no to someone's mum –

Paige I don't have time for this –

Gerald I bought you something. And look, I'm not unaware
this is an extremely weird thing to do, but –

Paige (*reading the cover*) A Thousand Years of Persian
Poetry –

Gerald It's mostly poems about gardens. And God. And
finding God in the garden. Or finding God in the garden
while you're drunk – Oh my God, ancient-Persian-poets
were drinking so much wine, but . . . I liked the modern
stuff . . . better, um . . . Can I?

*Gerald motions for the book and then flicks to a specific
page. He reads, awkward and unsure, from the
Farrokhzad poem 'Window' . . .*

Gerald
'When my trust hung suspended by the thin rope
    of justice
and all over town
they were chopping up the heart of my lamps
when they bound the childish eyes of my love
with the black blindfold of the law
and from the agitated temples of my desire
spurts of blood were scattering everywhere
when my life was nothing more
nothing more than the tick-tock of the wall clock
I realised I must, I must –'
(*Losing confidence.*) Anyway I liked that one the best –
Forugh Farrokhzad – you don't . . . you don't have to keep
it if you don't want to –

Paige (*joking*) Gerry, I . . . If I knew we were doing gifts,
then –

Gerald It's stupid, I know –

Paige No, it's . . .

Beat.

Actually, I . . . I think I do have something? I saw it last
week; I took a screenshot of it – I mean, it's no book of
poetry, but . . .

*She finds a picture on her phone, passes it over. Gerald
takes it . . . reluctantly.*

Go on, read it.

Gerald (*reading*) 'Matt and Stephanie Hughes . . . are proud
to announce the arrival of their second child . . . Gerald
Anthony Hughes.'

Beat. Paige grins.

Paige (*grinning*) It's a baby. Called Gerald. Like an actual –

Gerald No, no, I get it, yeah –

Paige Here, give me your number, I'll send you a copy. You can use it next time Nikki has a go at you –

Gerald This is all my fault.

Paige No, Gerry, it's really not –

Gerald This was *never* supposed to happen to you, okay?

Paige Yeah, well, it did so –

Gerald If I'd just told him to leave you alone, or . . . or said 'No', or . . . If I hadn't been such a fucking *coward* –

Paige Gerry, what are you talking about – ?

Gerald Aaron came up to me. That night. He came up to me and said: 'She wants to get with me, Gerry. Would you mind if I do that?'

Paige But . . . why would he have to ask your permission –

Gerald Because I picked you, didn't I?! A few days before you arrived, we had this list of all the freshers, and it was just . . . it was just a game, okay? It was just . . . It was just a stupid, *stupid* game, and I . . . I didn't really want to join in, but Aaron asked me to, and then I saw your photo, and it just . . . it hit me – (*Motioning to his chest.*) right here – like it just . . . it was so . . . it was so *powerful*, so I . . . I chose you. I decided . . . *you*. I had two weeks to make it happen. Until then, no one was supposed to touch you except for me, and, and maybe . . . maybe if I'd said something, Aaron would have left you alone –

Paige But I . . . I didn't know you.

Gerald No, I . . . I know –

Paige I gave you no indication that I liked you –

Gerald Yeah, but that's . . . that was kind of . . . that's the point of the game –

Paige No, I was *never* going to have sex with you –

Gerald Um . . . fucking hell, okay –

Paige I'm not attracted to you, Gerald – I have *zero* interest in sleeping with you – *zero* –

Gerald Okay – fuck – Paige – you don't have to be fucking *mean* about it, okay –

Paige YOU CHOSE ME FROM A LIST LIKE SOMETHING YOU CAN BUY –

SCENE EIGHT

Jo's office.

Jo Just you then?

Leila *Just* me –

Jo No Michael?

Leila No.

Jo So he's determined to hide behind emails –

Leila He can't be your friend at the moment, he needs to be Chair.

Jo And you? In what capacity are you visiting? Michael's proxy? Secret envoy for Nikki and Paige?

Leila I'm here as a friend.

Beat.

How many months did they offer to pay you out?

Jo The rest of the academic year.

Leila Ten months. Ten months is good.

Jo Is it?

Leila Should be enough time to find another job.

Jo And if I can't find another job?

Leila You will.

Jo I might not. In addition to being the most hated woman on the internet right now, I'm also the latter end of 'middle-aged'. One in isolation is difficult; two, I might as well shoot myself now –

Leila Well maybe you should have thought about that before you –

Jo I did. Unfortunately for me, my attachment to the principle of fairness has always trumped any desire to self-protect.

Have you seen how many times it's been shared – ?

Leila No –

Jo Thousands. Hundreds of thousands by now probably. Women, mostly. White . . . often. Mothers of boys, wives of men. There were also quite a few men. Quite a few . . . 'Men's Rights Activists' – gosh that was an interesting spin – You know who didn't sign it? People I fucking *respect*.

They phoned of course. 'I'm so glad you're speaking about this, Josie.' 'Thank you for being brave enough to write this, Jo.' 'I agree with your letter, Josie, but I hope you understand why I can't be seen to endorse it publicly.'

The irony isn't lost on me, by the way. For most of the nineties, I was accused of being far too radical – now, it seems, I'm not radical enough.

Leila You were never a radical, Jo. You were far too pragmatic.

Jo What's wrong with being pragmatic? A 'sensible revolutionary', a 'realistic dreamer', a 'practical idealist' –

Leila It doesn't exist –

Jo I'm here! I exist! While other people were weeping and wailing for Alison, I was the only one out there organising a protest, leading a vigil –

Leila You barely knew her –

Jo I knew you! I held *you*. Comforted *you*. We slept in the same tiny college bed for two weeks; a terrible thing happened, Leila, and I was your only friend who bothered to turn anger into action –

Leila Not for her. For this. (*Gesturing to the building.*) *This*. Unrestricted access to all of this, and you won, Josie – you won! You didn't reach the heights you wanted to, of course, but it's not your fault. We graduated in the eighties. We were promised a whole new wave of feminism, instead . . . we had the nineties. No one wanted to hear what you had to say. You weren't relevant any more – crop tops, computers, Spice Girls, *that* was relevant. And if you couldn't be relevant, you decided you'd be in charge, and you've done that, at least – we've both done that. I run the laboratory that Alison and I used to study in – you're head of an institution that forty years ago you wouldn't have been allowed to attend, but the minute you fear losing your position at the top, you wield the same power you used to fight against –

Jo Oh, that is *absurd* –

Leila You threatened Michael with sexual assault.

Beat.

Jo No . . . no –

Leila He told me what you said to him, Josie –

Jo I only . . . drew his attention to how a student-teacher relationship, back then, could now be re-interpreted –

Leila And you can't hear the threat in that?

Beat.

It has never bothered me that the two of you had
a relationship before he and I did. Never. If you hadn't
introduced me to him, I wouldn't have the life, the family,
the . . . the *love* I have now.

But your relationship was consensual . . . right? My
best friend would never knowingly set me up with a man
who . . . who *violated* her?

Josie . . . I need to know. Did Michael ever do anything
to make you feel uncomfortable – ?

Jo No.
I loved it.
I *loved* it.
I loved every dirty filthy fumbly fucking minute of it –
I loved fucking your husband, Leila – I *loved* it.

Silence.

Leila Well. Thank you for clarifying –

Jo Stay.
I need to pack a few things. Then I need to work out
which of these paintings belong to me, which belong to the
college, and then whether or not I care enough to make
the distinction, and then I suspect I'll need to eat. I can
steal a few of these college gift wines. I'll dig out the stash
of confiscated student weed I've been harbouring, and
then – if you let me make fun of you for taking up with
two student vigilantes – you, me, Michael – we can all get
royally-fucking-slaughtered –

Leila I've stopped working with them. I'd be grateful, Jo,
if you could hold off on visiting Michael and I, at least for
a while –

Jo How long – ?

Leila A while.

Beat.

Jo It's dangerous all this, isn't it? Something's begun. No one's quite sure where it's going, or where it will end, but it's likely to catch forty-nine per cent of the human population in its trawling net, and that . . . that is a lot of people we know and love –

Leila I don't give a shit about other people. I don't give a shit about other people's husbands, other people's children – I care about mine. My husband. My daughters –

Jo My goddaughter –

Leila Who need the only version of their father they've ever known and not the 'handsy professor' you, or any other misaligned young woman from his past, might try to concoct.

Pause.

Jo Thirty-eight years of friendship, Leila, clearly, if I'd wanted your love or loyalty, I should have married you – put one or two babies inside of you –

Leila turns to leave.

I need to mean something to you, Leila, I . . . You don't know what it's like to have to draw and – and constantly replenish your own personal fucking wellspring of – of confidence and self-esteem because you've been adored and loved by the same man since you were twenty-one years old, but for me, this is . . . You and I . . . *we* . . . this is the longest relationship I've ever had, and . . . and the irony is, Leila, I'm also the longest relationship you've ever had and –

Leila I don't like you, Jo.

Beat.

I'm sorry if that's shocking to hear, but . . . I don't.
I haven't liked you for . . . for a very long time.

Leila exits.
Silence.
If there's a single moment when Jo feels like crying, it's
probably this one, but instead, she looks for something to
steal, or break, or vandalise . . . she's not sure yet.
She remembers, somewhere, she still has the destroyed
painting of Winifred Heap.
As she returns from collecting it, Paige enters.
They stare at each other . . . Jo, painting in her hands.

Jo Winifred May Heap. I've been reading about her.

She played hockey. She collected shells. She campaigned
for twenty years for women to be admitted to this
university, and when the university conceded, on condition
suitable accommodation could be found, Winifred May
Heap fundraised for another two years and founded St
Claire's herself.

Personally, I've always believed that women should be
everywhere men are, and not cordoned off in 'suitable
accommodation', but maybe . . . maybe she wanted that.

(*Adding her to the pile.*) Regardless, Winnie, you're now
coming with me –

Paige So it's true then. They let you go.

Jo Oh, I wouldn't say that . . .

Paige What would you say?

Jo Apparently: 'Jo Mulligan has decided to leave for
personal reasons' –

Paige Have you – ?

Jo What do you want, Paige? It is, Paige, isn't it? We
haven't met properly of course, but I recognise you from the
video.

Paige You wrote me a letter.

Jo I wrote an open letter.

Paige Parts of it felt like they were for me.

Jo If you're looking for someone to be angry with, may I suggest you find someone who still works here –

Paige I'm leaving in a few hours. My mum will be here soon. My dad and my stepmum are already in town, but . . . they wanted a chance to speak to a lawyer first, so . . .

Jo Well, if they plan to sue, they may have to get in line . . .

Beat.

You don't know . . .

Paige Know what?

Jo Aaron's parents have filed charges.

Paige Against me –

Jo Against the college. For suspending him without due process.
    Don't worry. It won't go to court. The college will pay him out. Something substantial, I'm sure. And then there will be training programmes for staff . . . half a dozen haphazard consent workshops for students . . . a brief recommendation that all residential colleges review their formal misconduct policies, and they will, I'm sure . . . to further protect buildings like this . . . from young women like you.

Silence.

Paige What do I do now? I . . . I really need someone to tell me what to do –

Jo I can't be that person, Paige –

Paige What would you say to me if I was your daughter?

Jo Paige –

Paige Or friend? What would you say to me if I was your friend? Or . . . what would you tell me if I was you? Like . . . like a younger you? Did something like this ever happen to you – ?

Jo And why would I share that?

Paige I . . . I don't know, I –

Jo Unlike most people your age, I don't feel the need to share things, just – just 'because' –

Paige So it *has* happened to you –

Jo Yes. On my doorstep. A stranger jumped me from behind, pulled me into my own home. And then, in my first marriage, I hit my husband, so he dragged me to the bed. It seemed to shut me up okay, so he did it again, and as soon as it was over, I packed up my things, and I left.
　　None of that is true by the way.

Paige What?

Jo Not a single bit of it.

Paige You just . . . ? You just made that up – ?

Jo Maybe. Maybe I didn't. Either way, it doesn't belong to anyone but me.

Paige You're lucky then.

Jo 'Lucky' . . . okay –

Paige I don't feel like I have anything belongs to me –
I don't feel like I belong to me. I'm just . . . part of some story I never asked to be in, and the thing is, this story started before I even got here, I mean . . . I just found out some third-year guy chose me from a *list*, and –

Jo A list?

Paige A list of names. Incoming students. Apparently, the guys use the names to look up pictures of all the girls, and then they work out which ones they'll try to –

Jo (*heard enough*) Okay.

Jo may have to take a moment . . . turn, lean against something to process this, but Paige continues, oblivious.

Paige I worked so hard to be here. My mum and I, we . . . we drove all the way out here, years back, for . . . for motivation, something to . . . to aim for, and I decided *this* is the college I wanted to go to, and . . . I still do . . . I think. I want to go to my classes. I want to have arguments with my professors. I want to learn how to build these – these giant elaborate systems that help information travel all around the world – *I* want to travel the world. I want to make friends. I want to have sex that I remember. With a guy. With a girl, I think. I want to work out which I like better, or maybe I'll just keep having sex with both – I want to do all that and be anything other than that girl who got assaulted her first night of university.

Jo So do it.
Do it.
Leave the campaign. Remove your story. Pack it all away in a little box called 'shitty things that once happened to me', and forget about it –

Paige I *can't* –

Jo You can. You absolutely can –

Paige I can't –

Jo Why not –

Paige Because *I* don't want to let anyone down –

Jo Who?! Who would you be letting down – ?!

Paige Everyone –

Jo *Who – ?*

Paige Everyone! Everyone this has ever happened to, or – or will happen to – *people* – people who are never given the chance to be heard – everyone who was brave enough to send me their story – people who had it worse than me – so many people, like – like Nikki – *Nikki*, and – and that woman who was murdered, and – and fucking *Winifred Heap*, and . . .

> *Paige is too distressed to continue.*
> *Jo waits, allows silence and stillness to settle in.*
> *She studies Paige. From a distance.*
> *And then, with enormous difficulty . . .*

Jo If . . . If I had a daughter – (*Immediately hating the sentiment.*) Jesus Christ . . .

> *Beat. She tries again.*

If I had a daughter and . . . and she came to me, and said, 'Mum . . . a terrible thing happened to me' . . . What kind of parent would I be if I said, 'I'm sorry to hear that, my darling, because now this terrible thing is the only thing that matters. You are a victim. Wounded. Damaged. And the psychological trauma of this is going to haunt you, and your experiences, and your future relationships, very possibly, for the rest of your life.' If I said that . . . to this hypothetical daughter of mine . . . that would be a form of cruelty, I think.

So I will say this.

A terrible thing happened to you, Paige. But it doesn't need to be absolved with . . . with obligatory acts of service, and it certainly doesn't define you. It doesn't. It just . . . doesn't. And I'm sorry I don't know you better, because if I did, I might be able to back that statement up with one or two tangible examples, but what I do know is that you are not even halfway through becoming all the things you're going to be, and that is *exciting*.

You worked to be here. You *deserve* to be here. So stay and plumb this grand building for everything it's worth. You'll go to classes, make friends, argue with professors. You'll learn who you are. You'll learn who you want to be next. You'll fuck some men – fuck some women – you'll learn what you like, what you don't like, and then you'll learn to ask for what you *want*, and without apology, and you do not need to wait for someone like me to give you permission.

But maybe take a bottle of wine. Or a monogrammed fountain pen. I've spent all day trying to fleece this building of everything I can, and to be honest I'm not entirely sure how I'm going to get it all out of here.

Paige moves over to a box. Takes out a token bottle of wine. Tucks a monogrammed fountain pen in her pocket for good measure. Whatever feels right.

Thank you.

Jo You really don't have to thank me –

Paige Thank you. *Thank you.*

Paige exits, lighter somehow.
Jo remains, looks around her office and then at the odd collection of things she's pillaged.
She pulls out a lighter. Waves it over the pile, briefly considers burning it, perhaps the whole building with it . . . but instead . . . she takes out the stash of confiscated student weed, lights a pre-rolled joint . . . and enjoys it.

Night. The college sportsground.
  Nikki, dirty, dishevelled, sweaty, with a haphazardly dug-out tree. Perhaps it's already there, perhaps she's dragging it on a tarpaulin, or a purloined shopping cart, or some such. However the tree arrives or appears, it's obviously not part of some elaborate plan, just a spur-of-the-moment, emotion-fuelled decision by Nikki.
  Gerald appears, some beer in hand, ready to kick a football around.

Gerald Just to let you know –

Nikki (*startled*) Holy fucking shit.

Gerald If you can believe it, I was genuinely trying to avoid that. I fake-coughed a bit . . . back there –

Nikki Look, can you just get wrecked somewhere else, please?

Gerald No.

Nikki No?

Gerald You don't own the sports ground, Nikki – it belongs to everyone –

  Nikki ignores him – takes out a shovel –

Whoa – okay – okay, Nikki, you can't just . . . Nikki . . . Nikki, *stop* – do you not understand how much work it takes to maintain a sports pitch – ?!

  Nikki lets out a guttural roar of frustration . . . at the barely broken ground, at Gerald, at just . . . everything.
  Silence.
  Then she continues digging.
  Gerald moves over to the tree, still lying on its side. He picks up the small plaque that used to sit in front of it. Reads it.

You know the ground staff are just going to put it back in the morning –

Nikki Then I'll move it again.

Gerald And then they'll put it back –

Nikki And then I'll dig it up again, and again, and again, and I'll do it every week until I graduate if I have to, and by that point, maybe it becomes a tradition, because these places . . . they love a tradition . . . especially one that makes zero fucking sense, and if students can go on an annual magic-goose hunt, or drink beer out of an iron shoe, or touch the left boob of that one statue when they finish their final exams, then maybe they'll want to dig up a dead woman's tree, and replant it somewhere people can actually see it, not in some tiny out-of-the-way corner, where no ever stops to read the stupid fucking plaque and –

Gerald (*re the plaque*) 'Alison Welsh. Beloved daughter. Cherished friend. 1967 to 1986.'

Beat.

Do you want some help?

Nikki No.

Gerald Are you sure? Because maybe I could –

Nikki No.

> *Nikki continues digging, focused and determined.*
> *Gerald, unsure what to do . . . doesn't do anything.*
> *He opens a beer and drinks a bit of it.*
> *He considers walking back to the college.*
> *Decides against it.*
> *He starts nudging the ball around.*
> *After a few moments, he opens another beer for Nikki, places it where she can see it, and then returns to the football.*
> *Nikki glances at the beer – and at Gerald – but continues digging.*

Some distance away, Jo appears on her way out of the building. She carries a bag or box of essentials perhaps, but the only other item she's chosen to take with her is the portrait of Winifred, now tucked under her arm.

Jo pauses to watch as Nikki attempts to drag the tree to the freshly dug hole.

From Jo, a glimmer of something . . . recognition, perhaps . . . pride, even.

It becomes clear that Nikki needs help. Gerald offers without ceremony. Nikki accepts without gratitude.

Nikki takes a moment to retrieve the beer – but spies Jo . . . leaving.

From Nikki, a glimmer of something . . . recognition, perhaps . . . a little sadness, maybe . . . but given the weight of everything she's still holding, ultimately far too complex to be felt or displayed as easy sentiment.

Jo exits.

Nikki drinks.

Nikki returns to the tree.

And before Nikki and Gerald manage to raise it –

End of play.